The Secret Police of Russia

*Neglectful Treatment, Cooperation,
and Giving in
(2022 Guide for Beginners)*

Marc Booth

TABLE OF CONTENT

Introduction   1

Chapter One: The Early Year of KGB-CHEKA   5

Chapter Two: The KGB'S Early Years – GPU   13

Chapter three: the KGB'S early years – OGPU   16

Chapter Four: The NKVD and the birth of the KGB   24

Chapter Five: How Stalin's NKVD Spies took down Trotsky   36

Chapter Six: The Fall of a Superpower - The Fall of the Soviet Union   58

Chapter Seven: How Novichok Was used as a Political Tool   77

Introduction

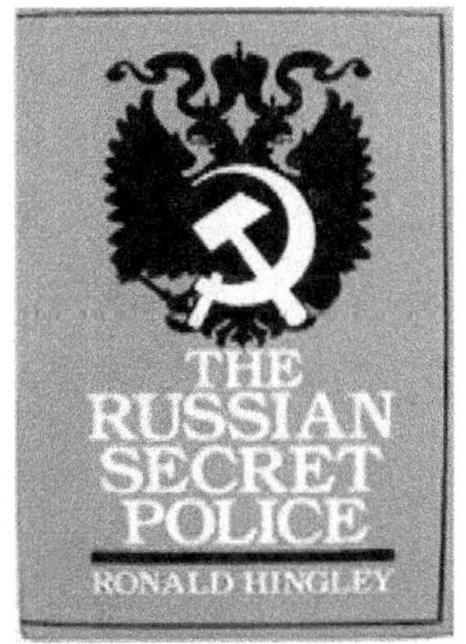

This book is about the history of the KGB, its leaders, and propaganda and accomplishment throughout the last 105 years you will learn how the since the first secret police, the KGB has terrorized the Soviet people. Cheka was created. Even though the Cheka was disbanded in 1922, they continued to exist, responsible for policing multiple labor camps and the Gulag system allegedly carrying out approximately 250,000 executions The Cheka was renamed after that.

GPU, OGPU, NKVD, KGB, FSK, and FSB are all examples. Each secret police force. They carried on what Cheka had started at home, but they also established several spymasters and dispatched them around the world to provide information to the Soviet Union each Unit was charged with some of the same responsibilities as the Department of Today's Homeland Security in the United States protects.

They were accountable for protecting the country from both local and foreign dangers, how many major historical events occurred in both the First and Second World Wars, as well as slaughtering and executing millions of people both locally and internationally as well as internationally you will study the demise of superpowers, as well as the demise of the Soviet Union. Finally, you will learn how the most recent instance of the Russian Secret Service employing Novick as a political tool Instrument. As you can see, this book covers everything.

Before embarking on this voyage, let us first grasp why the KGB exists. Even today, such a ferocious reputation! Why is the KGB so feared?

A recent British investigation into the strange death of a former KGB agent. Alexander Litvinenko, a Russian intelligence agent, concluded that Russian President Vladimir Putin most likely authorized his assassination. While the situation is unknown whether or whether these claims are valid, the suppression of opposition is not unavoidable. Logo for the KGB, the former Soviet security agency but what about what precisely was the KGB, and why was it so feared back then? So, the KGB, or "Kumite Gosudarstvennoy Bezopasnosti," was the Soviet secret police. The security and foreign intelligence agency of the European Union. It was operational from 1954 until 1991. When the Soviet Union fell apart, it was succeeded by

In the new Russian Federation, the FSK was followed by the FSB. They both have similarities to the KGB in terms of security throughout its life, unlike other countries' security organizations, the KGB was practically an international organization. The organization was responsible for a variety of tasks, including intelligence collection, border security, and propaganda enforcement. However, most notably, it served as Russia's domestic surveillance unit and secret police More than 500,000 people.

The KGB employed thousands of international citizens. It was the largest institution of its sort at the time. The KGB obtained intelligence all around the world by using "legitimate" means". Resident spies" were Soviet citizens granted permission to stay in the country. Other countries by working in embassies or comparable positions at international levels would be able to claim diplomatic immunity. If caught, immunity is granted. Russia too has undocumented spies with no immunity and, despite the higher risk, they were able to integrate more easily without prompt suspicion domestically, the KGB was regarded with suspicion.

The secret police of the country would go after those accused of being anti-communist or anti-government, and search regularly Dissidents are arrested and their residences are searched. They created individual religious activities control departments, subversive nationalism Foreign influence, illegal media, and, in particular, the Jewish media population.

The KGB even conducted operations against heads of state. Posted a danger to the stability of Soviet ideology Former and current actors KGB officers staged what was deemed a nonviolent takeover d'état of Soviet leader Nikita Khrushchev, who was replaced by Brezhnev, Leonid However, the KGB's next coup attempt failed. Mikhail Gorbachev was President of

Russia in 1991. As Gorbachev began to enact changes, he was detained by the KGB. The KGB was afraid of losing power. Even though the coup failed after two attempts.

It has recently been identified as a major contributor to the rapid that same year, the Soviet Union was destabilized and collapsed. The KGB was a long-feared organization and a major source of suspicion. A source of concern for the United States during the Cold War even though the present Russian President presided over the dissolution of the Soviet Union. From 1975 to 1991, Vladimir Putin served as a KGB officer. It is why many people wonder if its influence and tactics of it are debatable the KGB is gone from the Russian government. The problem in the political sphere Alexander Litvinenko's death was tragic

Chapter One

The Early Year of KGB-CHEKA

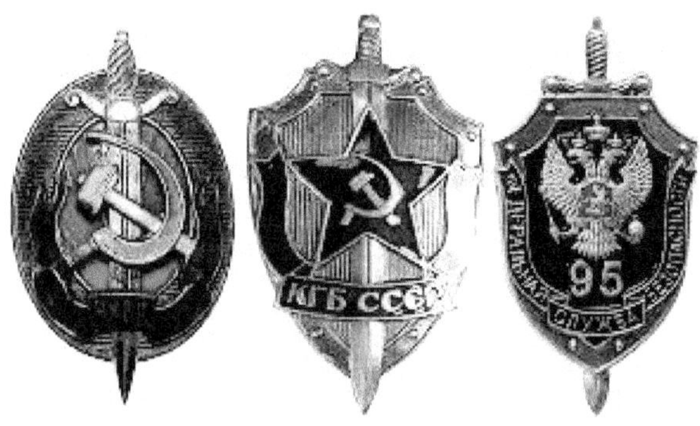

The KGB is one of the most effective security agencies in the world. The former Soviet Union's State Security Committee, known as the KGB, was disbanded in 1991. Turansky Square, in front of the KGB headquarters in Moscow, was named for the first Bolshevik security commander. It is currently known as Lubyanka, its original name. The KGB is associated with secrecy, dread, and evil. For more than 70 years, the Soviet security organization operated under several titles and was a strong and authoritarian body feared by the entire Soviet populace. An examination of the KGB's background reveals information about its origins. The KGB and its predecessors have played significant roles in Russian history. The Bolsheviks required a secret police agency following the October Revolution. Their party was small and unpopular, and it appeared that they could lose power just as easily as they had gained it. On December 7, 1917, the Soviet People's Commissars, at Lenin's request, founded the all-Russian special Commission for fighting counter-revolution and sabotage of the dreaded Cheka.

Felix Dzerzhinsky was named chairman. Dzerzhinsky was born in 1877 to a poor Polish nobleman's family and had a religious education. He joined the revolutionaries in his teens and was often arrested and imprisoned. In 1906, he was elected to the Bolshevik Central Committee, and he was a member of the military Revolutionary Committee that oversaw the events of October 1917. Dzerzhinsky was adamant that the Bolshevik cause must triumph at any cost. He was known as both the most honest knight of the revolution and the General Inquisitor. Stalin's assessment of him was "There was no name more despised by the Bourgeoisie than his." The Cheka's chairman has almost no personnel or dependable agents. Only a few of the initial 20 men would survive, including Yakov Peters, Ivanka Senafrontoff, and Martin Latsis. The Bolsheviks delegated numerous crucial tasks to the Cheka. Russia awaited the Constituent Assembly to convene and build the groundwork for a new political structure. Many people hoped that this would be the end of it.

Opposing parties prepared for a parliamentary battle in the face of

Bolshevik dominance. However, the Bolsheviks had no intention of ceding power to the duly elected Assembly. Cheka agents arrested Union members in December 1917 for supporting the Constituent Assembly. On January 5, 1918, Bolshevik soldiers suppressed a rally of its sympathizers. The Assembly met in Torrid's palace. The next day, security led by Cheka agents block delegates from entering the building. That night, inebriated red guards savagely murdered two delegates, André Zengariof and Fodor Kukushkin, who had been imprisoned earlier.

The murder rocked the country, and the Cheka was forced to apprehend the two murderers, but they went unpunished, and the matter was closed. This episode foreshadowed what was to come. The Cheka would become an expert in crowd control and violent death. The situation for the Bolsheviks was precarious. The Soviet republic was on the verge of military collapse in February 1918, and Petrograd was under threat. "The Soviet motherland is in jeopardy," Lenin declared. The Cheka agents have arrived. Hostile agents, thugs, speculators, counter-revolutionary agitators, and German spies might be shot on the spot The Cheka may carry out executions.

There was no need for proof of guilt. This enabled them to maintain rigorous discipline in the Red Army's rear. Some were criminals who posed little threat to the Bolshevik dictatorship, but the vast majority were political opponents who posed a considerably greater threat to the revolution. The summer of 1918 was a particularly bloody moment in the Bolshevik drive for full political control, and the Cheka once again played an important role. The 5th Congress of Soviets gathered in Moscow on July 4th. The political party led by Maria Spiridonova, the left SRs, strongly condemned the Bolsheviks. The Cheka struck back. On July 6, Yakov Boomkin, a member of the left SR party and a checker agent, killed Count Minibar. Lenin accused the leftists of trying to start a war with Germany. When Dzerzhinsky attempted to apprehend the assassin, he discovered that several Cheka members were loyal to the leftists and refused to follow his orders. He and other Bolshevik leaders were apprehended, and combat ensued. The odds were stacked against the SRs.

Two days later, reinforcements and the deputy of Dzerzhinsky, Yaakov Peters, put down the rebellion and arrested our Marxist leaders. Merbau Skillah worked for the Cheka for a long time. The Bolsheviks had solidified political power as a result of the July upheaval, but it was not yet secure. Terrorism was organized as the next stage. Dzerzhinsky describes it as "an utterly natural aspect of the revolution." The Bolsheviks waited for the right moment to unleash the Red Terror.

On August 30th, a major member of the Petrograd regional Cheka was assassinated. Lenin was shot and wounded in Moscow, and the Soviets were accused of both attacks. Many historians believe the attacks were sponsored by the Cheka because retribution was so swift and well-organized. With no accurate information about the incident and an hour after Lenin was injured, Yakov Sverdlov declared that the working class will retaliate with mass terror against all enemies of the revolution. "The Bourgeoisie can kill some people; we can destroy a whole class," stated Grigory Zinoviev, leader of the Petrograd Soviet. 500 hostages were shot in Petrograd shortly after your

Itsuki's death and the declaration of Red Terror. The country was hit by a surge of executions. Local Cheka battalions comprised solely of Bolsheviks were becoming incredibly effective. The all-Russian extraordinary commission gradually infiltrated every aspect of society. Small towns and outlying areas were given offices. Mikail Petrov was appointed chief of the Special Department to combat counter-revolution and espionage in the Army and Navy in February 1919.

The Cheka now possessed its huge military forces. The list of offenses for which the checker could impose punishment was increased. The Cheka's fearsome strength had practically no bounds. Dzerzhinsky installed and reviewed the eastern front with him in early 1919. They agreed on the significance of the secret police organization and recognized its potential. The Bolsheviks' political opponents were not yet petrified by fear of the Cheka. A large bomb exploded in downtown Moscow-street on September 25, 1919. The 50-pound charge destroyed the building where the Moscow party committee was meeting. Moscow Bolshevik leader Vladimir Zagorski and 11 others were killed, while 55 were injured. Trotsky and Kamenev were both eulogized. The deceased meanwhile, the Cheka had launched its investigation. Dzerzhinsky initially suspected the SR party in the national center of being behind the bombing. Hundreds more members of these organizations who were being held on unrelated charges were promptly shot.

However, detectives led by Moscow Cheka commander Vasily Mansaf soon discovered that the anarchist underground was responsible. Secret apartments, publishing facilities, and explosives workshops were all destroyed in two weeks. No one called the erroneous killings into question. Most Cheka our folks did not think they were a mistake.

Even among the Bolsheviks, no one dared to publicly challenge the Cheka, though they secretly remarked that their motto "All power to the Soviets" had been transformed to "All power to the Cheka." Many people believed that the Soviet Union's dire military and political position warranted this. Every Civil War triumph had become routine. Discontent pervaded the land and erupted everywhere. The outbursts were dubbed "counter-revolutionary conspiracies" by the Bolsheviks. Iron was given vital new tasks by Lenin.

Felix, who was still the Cheka's leader, was also appointed People's Commissar for Home Affairs. Simultaneously, he resolved labor conscription difficulties and oversaw the commissariat for communication means.

The Cheka ruled over the frontier guards. Dzerzhinsky afterward got involved in diplomatic matters and was a member of the Science Committee. His Secret Service was in charge of all essential state concerns. The Chekas' principal targets were not the opponents of the working class, but everyone hostile to Bolshevism. Beginning in 1918, the Soviets seized excess grain from peasants. Cheka Food units used special weapons to force compliance and often completely depleted villages of all provisions. Those who attempted to conceal bread or grain were executed on the spot.

Peasant revolts became prevalent. Peasants in the Tambov region, led by Alexandre Antonov, waged guerilla warfare against the Bolsheviks from 1929 to 1921. The Soviet government retaliated with punitive raids, and ordinary Red Army troops battling Antonov were bolstered with special Cheka attachments, including Dzerzhinsky's armored vehicle unit. Rebel relatives were kidnapped, and a network of detention camps was established.

Rising throughout the region Families of guerrillas who refused to surrender were deported or executed. The climax came in the summer of 1921 when our agents entered Antonov's headquarters and the peasant rebellion was savagely repressed. That same year, the Bolsheviks faced another challenge: an uprising by sailors from the Naval Base at Constant. When the Cheka attack failed to subjugate the insurgent sailors, army forces decided the outcome.

The Cheka completed the task. Many insurgents were killed, while others were imprisoned or exiled. In 1921, Russia faced a terrible famine that killed 5 million people. The Volga region's people ate grass, and cannibalism was documented. Peasants abandoned their communities in an attempt to survive. The civilized world was astonished and attempted to assist. Anatole France's Nobel Prize was donated to hunger relief. The American Relief Administration was established to provide food to Russia. Fiji Nansen, a Norwegian polar explorer, visited the starving zones and advocated for a relief effort, but the Cheka was persuaded that aid efforts were only cloaks for espionage. Even during official events, personnel of the American Relief Administration was under constant Cheka observation. Many people were arrested. The Russian Orthodox Church, led by Patriarch Tikhon, raised funds for the hungry peasants. However, the Bolsheviks were concerned that this might undermine their authority and hence prohibited the church's efforts.

The Soviet government subsequently established the State Committee for Famine Relief, which requested that the church surrender all treasures not needed for religious services. In reality, the Cheka was behind this requisition of all church riches. Patriarchy Tecum unsuccessfully petitioned the government and attempted to complain to Lenin about the Cheka's oppression. He was not aware of Lenin's message to all local authorities, in which he urged them to close all churches and execute as many priests as possible. The Patriarch's tenacity led to his house arrest, further incarceration in the Donskoy Monastery, and, ultimately, his untimely death in 1925.

Chapter Two

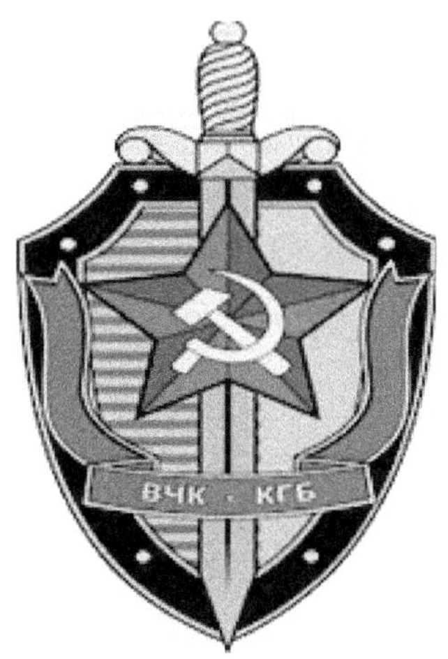

The Orthodox Church was virtually totally controlled by the state at the time. Most churches were destroyed or desecrated after eight years of Bolshevik control. Only seven of Petrograd's 96 churches remained open. Thousands of socially foreign clergymen were interned in the monasteries. The church's assets, worth millions of gold rubles, were absorbed by the State Treasury but were never used for famine relief. Other methods were preferred by the Bolsheviks. A special Cheka our train was dispatched from Moscow to Siberia, carrying food Raiders led by Suzuki himself. His aides were given the authority to requisition food by any means and carry it back to European Russia. Dzerzhinsky was no longer the Cheka's chairman when he returned from his bread expedition in February 1922. He was now the chairman of the GPU, which had been founded within the people's commissariat for Home Affairs, the NKVD. With the Civil War's end, the Bolsheviks attempted to demonstrate that the Cheka's enormous capabilities were no longer required. The most significant aspect was political administration. The Soviet regime annihilated those who publicly opposed them and sought hidden opponents.

Dzerzhinsky's response was straightforward: the GPU should become a reincarnation of the Cheka's glorious accomplishments and traditions. He prepared a trial against the imprisoned SR leaders in the summer of 1922. This was a forerunner to Stalin's show trial in the 1930s. The trial was presided upon by Yogi Pietàcoffe. Prosecutors were Nicolai Alenko and Anatole Lunacharsky. The majority of them in the Supreme Court Hall was GPU agents dressed in civilian attire. The GPU painstakingly prepared for the trial, and several of the prisoners pled guilty under duress, implicating their old comrades, members of the SS Central Committee. Grigory Semyonov and Lidia Konoplyova, two provocateurs, had entered this obedient gang. The prosecution had a tight grip on Nikolai Bukharin, who represented this group.

The charges, which ranged from inciting a civil war to an attempt to assassinate Lenin, were false. Nonetheless, Kurylenko wanted the execution penalty. Things did not go as planned. The trial's planners were disappointed. The defendants remained unfazed and refused to confess. They refused to plead guilty, accusing the Bolshevik regime of political oppression and witnessing abuse.

The death penalty was not approved by the government. Lev Kamenev proposed that the execution be postponed indefinitely, and the 12 SRs became life prisoners. The SR trial was a humiliation for the GPU, which was to be more successful in the work of the Commission for the Improvement of Children's Lives, created in 1921 and led by the untiring Dzerzhinsky. Dzerzhinsky, according to people's commissar for education Lunacharsky, considered that the commissariat for education was insufficient and required Cheka competence. The situation was really serious. Civil war retaliation and forced migrations resulted in a large number of orphans. Six million of these orphaned children roamed Russia's streets and clogged its towns. Cheka's goals in establishing the commission were not just to enhance children's living conditions, but also to reduce juvenile criminality. The Cheka GPU oversaw the construction of special orphanages throughout Russia. They supplied housing, clothing, food, and basic education. Most importantly, the children were overly controlled. Juvenile delinquents were sent to a reformatory, where labor was the most common form of punishment. Anton McCarranca oversaw the most notorious reformatory, named after Felix Deschinsky.

CHAPTER THREE

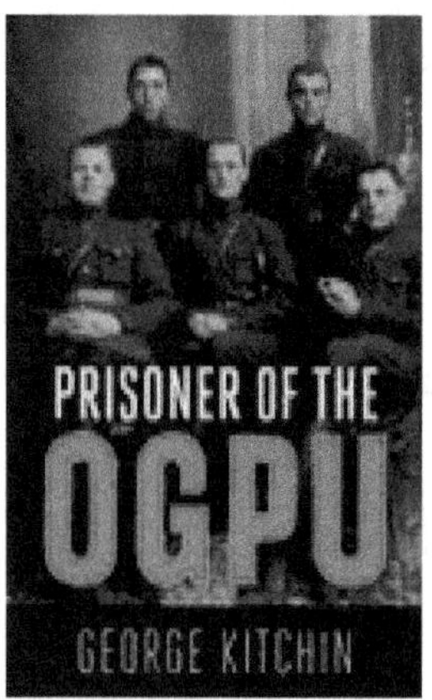

The Soviet Union commemorated the fifth anniversary of their secret service in December 1922. When Michael Kalinin spoke, crack GPU troops paraded across Red Square, and the major celebration was staged at the Bolshoi Theatre. "The entire human race owes it to the Cheka," he remarked. Deschinsky was bestowed with the first badge of an honorable Cheka officer. When the newly formed USSR's first Congress of Soviets convened a few days later, the Party Central Committee decided to rename the Secret Service once more. The GPU was renamed the OGPU (United States Political Agency). This agency aimed to keep an eye not only on Russia but on the entire Soviet Union. Deschinsky was appointed to the Soviet cabinet. From then on, all secret police chiefs would be appointed to the highest levels of the party and state. The OGPU encountered various opponents outside the USSR in 1923. The enemy used terrorist attacks on occasion, and famous Soviet diplomat Vatslat Ferozky was shot point blank in LaSalle. The OGPU, known for its terrorist techniques in Russia, condemned the murder and organized a public demonstration against political assassination. After 1922, the West struggled to deal with OGPU international intelligence, which was led by Mikail Trellis. Although Soviet influence was particularly strong in Persia and Afghanistan, the OGPU's principal aim was within the Soviet Union. Lenin was gravely ill, and the selection of a successor was vital. As the leadership struggle inside the party heated up, the biggest competitors appeared to be Lekf Rotsky, Nikolai Bukharin, Left Kamenev, Grigory Zinoviev, and Mikail Tomsky.

However, only three persons possessed genuine power. Trotsky was in charge of the Red Army, Deschinsky of the OGPU, and Stalin of the party apparatchiks. Stalin and Deschinsky were united in their hatred of Trotsky. Deschinsky labeled Trotsky's supporters as party opponents who had no place in the OGPU in December 1923. Lenin died on January 21, 1924. During the six days that followed, as the Soviet people mourned the death of the Bolshevik leader, the Party Central Committee chose who would wield power. Deschinsky presided over the Commission for the funeral of Lenin. He took over the Supreme Soviet of People's Economy five days later, without resigning from his primary role as head of the OGPU. Stalin remained the Bolshevik Party's, General Secretary. Lenin was vehemently opposed, but with the assistance of the OGPU, his last will was hidden from the public.

Party membership. The political agency had grown into a well-organized institution by 1924, with hundreds of thousands of official and civilian employees. Secret personnel, a plethora of services and departments, and a sizable contingent of troops that out-equip and train most red army divisions. Including the costs of sustaining military units and border guards, the OGPU's annual budget was four million golden rubles. Foreign intelligence had a three-million-dollar budget. OGPU agents had access to exclusive stores with high-quality products as well as lavish apartments.

The OGPU men saw themselves as a selected group, a state within a state. At the same time, they were given particular orders to conduct political propaganda among the populace and establish firm contact with them to bolster the OGPU's authority. Many Soviet organizations provided formal support to the OGPU units, as directed from on high. This exemplified the unshakable bond that existed between the people and the secret service. The Soviet secret service was able to carry out multiple successful operations because of generous funding and a wealth of experience. One of the most famous was the arrest in 1924 of Barres Savankov, a long-time Soviet foe. Savankov, a member of the Soviet fighting organization,

Since 1918, he has lived in exile, hoping for a change of fortune for the anti-Bolshevik forces. The OGPU started looking for Savankov. From Hundreds of people were arrested and prosecuted associated with him from 1921 to 1924. Some of them betrayed the Soviet leader, but Savankov could not be persuaded to return to Soviet territory unless he was granted leadership of a bogus clandestine outfit. Artur Artistsoff, the OGPU counterintelligence chief, is in charge of the Syndicate 2 operation. Andrei Fyodor, an undercover operative, traveled abroad disguised as an anti-Bolshevik. He persuaded Savankov that Russians were waiting for him at the border. Following the crossing of the border by Savankov and his colleagues, Deputy Puglia had them detained in Minsk. The court issued a stunning decision. Savankov was sentenced to years in prison rather than execution. However, in May 1925, he fell from a prison window. His death was considered suicide by the OGPU.

Stalin increased his position in 1925. His most crucial maneuver was the deposition of Trotsky as Red Army chief, but his successor, Mikhail Franza, proved to be too autonomous and powerful for Stalin's comfort. Franza died during surgery that year, which was convenient. He was recommended not to have the surgery, and it was never mentioned in later medical reports. There were connections between the secret police and the doctors. Clemente Voroshilov, who was passionately loyal to Stalin, was assigned command of the Red Army, but Voroshilov had been one of Cheka's early agents. Another pivotal power struggle occurred in the party in 1925. Sergei Kirov became secretary of the Leningrad City party organization, with Deschinsky's active assistance. He took over as leader of the new opposition, Grigory Zinoviev, who was determined to limit Stalin's rising political authority.

Many historians believe that in the closing months of his life, Deschinsky grew increasingly fearful of Stalin, although his final public appearance was in support of the general secretary. On July 20, 1926, at the Central Committee plenum, he would condemn Stalin's opponent, Kamenev. Deschinsky, however, fainted soon following his remarks. The doctor was delayed in some way.

Deschinsky would die two hours later in the arms of his subordinate, Abramble Enki. The funeral of Deschinsky was a significant event for the Bolsheviks. All of the party leaders marched together one last time. Each man's position in the honor guard indicated his political clout. As they buried Deschinsky, the Bolsheviks said goodbye not only to a comrade but to an era - the epoch of idealistic revolutionary terror had come to an end. On July 30, 1926, Purchase Loughman Menschinsky was appointed Chairman of the OGPU.

Menschinsky was born in 1874, attended Petersburg University, and joined the Bolsheviks in 1902. Menschinsky became People's Commissar for Finance after the October coup, and later Russia's General Council in Berlin. He was assigned to the Cheka in 1919 and eventually became Dzerzhinsky's deputy. Menschinsky was distinct from his colleagues. He belonged to the intelligentsia and was a master in physics and chemistry. He was interested in astronomy and spoke 20 languages. He was also a gentleman, which seemed to be a significant liability for someone in his position. Menschinsky was regarded by Trotsky as a shadow of a man, but this was exactly what Stalin required. Stalin became the true and total master of the OGPU after the appointment of Menschinsky.

General Yagoda, Menschinsky's and Stalin's second-in-command. The OGPU was present at every stage of Stalin's terror regime. The country was undergoing industrialization. The lofty goals and arbitrary timelines were unattainable.

Construction projects' careful planning and the hard effort of ordinary workers were undermined by instability, mismanagement, and chronic shortages of even the most basic materials. The party's inexperienced and ineffective red directors could hardly be blamed. Instead, the Bolsheviks sought a scapegoat. The OGPU came up with a solution. Bourgeois specialists blamed slow industrial development on sabotage. The title was given to seasoned engineers who did not support Bolsheviks. In 1928, a group of seasoned engineers from the Donetsk ole Basin was unjustly accused of counter-revolutionary activities and jailed.

The OGPU's manufactured Shakti Case was one of the first show trials. Stalin was dissatisfied with the outcome. Only 16 of the 58 defendants entered pleas of guilty. Despite extensive investigations, prosecutor Nikolai Kirilenko was unable to produce conclusive evidence of the defendant's serious crimes. The Supreme Court, led by Andre Wyszynski, sentenced 11 engineers to death, but the government refused to sanction the punishment, resulting in their imprisonment. Crylenko and the OGPU worked on a fresh case for two years. Saboteurs were now being exposed throughout the Soviet industries. Opposition party members were removed from every Enterprise, and those lacking proletariat origins were condemned.

After being tried in open courts, they were remanded to the OGPU Commission and sent to prisons and work camps. Yakov Peters led the Central Commission for Purges. The phony trial of the non-existent industrial party the prom partier took place late in the 1930s. The OGPU made amends for previous errors. There were just eight defendants in total. The majority of them sincerely admitted to making mistakes committing crimes and testifying for the prosecution

The OGPU pressured Professor Leonid Ramzan, the putative leader of Krampus here, and the seven other defendants into confessing. Other defendants who were less cooperative were slain. In a show of mercy to those who confessed, the death penalty was imposed, but it was eventually lowered to ten years in prison. At the same time, Russian peasants faced terrible retaliation. Stalin's collectivization began in 1928 with the first stage. Millions of peasants who refused to join the collective farms were persecuted. Exiled were the gulags or wealthy peasants. Gulags could be considered for any peasant. This heist was disguised as a fight against the gulags. Villages had been abandoned, and prisons were overcrowded. Stalin conceived a new scheme to build socialism using slave labor. Convicts would be exploited and discarded.

The Ministry of Justice's prisons and camps were subordinated to the OGPU. The infamous gulag, the main camp administration, arose from this. Its first leader was Henry Yagoda. The gulag was tested at Soloffky. In 1923, a model concentration camp was established on the grounds of the barren and ruined Soloffky monastery, which was located on islands miles offshore in the freezing White Sea. There was no touch with the mainland during the six-month winters. Inmates were publicly ridiculed and harassed, as well as assaulted and tortured. Many people were executed without a trial.

The basic economic premise of the gulags was tested at Soloffky to extract the most labor at the lowest cost. The Soloffky camp generated 63000 rubles of lumber in 1926. In 1929, the sum had risen to 3.5 million rubles, and a year later, it had dropped to million rubles.

Convict numbers climbed from 3000 in 1923 to 50000 in 1930. Labor productivity improved tenfold. This was the economics of the Gulag. However, even on a massive scale, timber harvesting had little political impact. Stalin desired a massive construction project that could be completed swiftly and cheaply. In September 1931, work on a canal connecting the White and Baltic oceans began. Thousands of prisoners would be sacrificed for this massive undertaking, which would be overseen by the OGPU.

Chapter Four

The NKVD and the Birth of the KGB

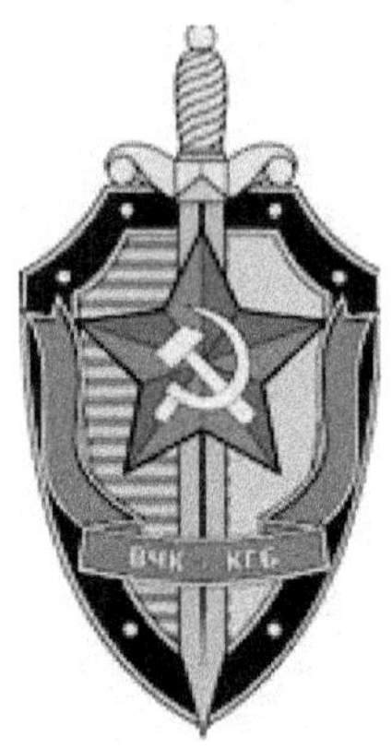

Yagoda was 43 years old and an engraver's apprentice when he became a professional revolutionary in 1934. His marriage to Yakov Sverdlov's niece insured a rapid climb in the party hierarchy. In 1920, he joined the Cheka. He had controlled all domestic OGPU operations as Manschinsky's deputy, and Stalin had never questioned Yagoda's devotion. Yagoda took over not only the OGPU, but also the police frontier guards, camps, jails, and fire brigades, which were all subordinated to the newly formed People's Commissariat for Internal Affairs, or NKVD. The public's access to information concerning NKVD activities was restricted. Appeals to raise popular support for the NKVD were not withdrawn. Newsreels show border guards standing guard along the world's longest land border. All other actions were kept under wraps. Yagoda's first action was to establish special conferences, which were punitive committees with the authority to sign death sentences without ever meeting the defendant. The unique meetings were dubbed "rapid-fire justice."

The state's genocidal policy increased and escalated. Stalin required an excuse to unleash the most massive terror campaign in history. He won it on December 1, 1934, when SergeiKirovv was shot in the party headquarters in Leningrad. Initially, his death was blamed on a deranged member of a fictitious sabotage group. In actuality, the assassination was planned by the NKVD's Leningrad Department under Stalin's orders. When all possible witnesses to the killing were murdered, evidence that an NKVD hitman fired the fatal shot vanished. Stalin would subsequently blame Kirov's death on his main political opponents, Grigory Zinoviev and Lev Kamenev. Both were tried and sentenced to five years in work camps on January 15, 1935.

Even though there was no proof involved. The big dread had started. Nikolai Azov, Secretary of the Party Central Committee, began planning the first Moscow trial in 1936. The defendants were accused of being part of a massive anti-Stalinist conspiracy that reportedly linked other leaders of the routed resistance to Trotsky. The trial concluded in August 1936 with all defendants to face the death penalty. In the weeks that followed, thousands of people were convicted in special NKVD tribunals for being disloyal to the regime. Many foreign communists living in the Soviet Union were detained. Yagoda bolstered international espionage. The Spanish Civil War provided the ideal opportunity for NKVD spies to eliminate dissenters among Communist International members.

Foreign communists opposed to Stalin who had enlisted to fight in Spain were identified and covertly executed during the war. The NKVD prepared for the second Moscow trial in the second half of 1936, by Stalin's directive. Those arrested were charged with being leaders of a parallel center. If the plot failed, the center allegedly planned to launch a terror campaign. Among the 17 defendants was Grigory's former Finance Minister's colleague. Yogi Pietàcoug, a former heavy industry chief, Carl Radek, a well-known journalist, and others. Thirteen innocent people were executed in NKVD dungeons on January 30, 1937. Sergei Jonnakinsey, People's Commissar for Heavy Industry, died unexpectedly three weeks later.

As Stalin's closest collaborator and personal friend, he felt free to criticize Stalin's decisions. Yagoda's absence from Jonnakinsey's burial exposed Yagoda's loss of power. The security chief was relegated to the minor post of commissar for communication in October 1936. Nikolai Jesof, a persistent drunkard, was appointed as the new chief of the NKVD. He was physically challenged, cruel, and had a penchant for singing.

The worst time in Soviet history had only barely begun. The former NKVD personnel was Europe's first casualties. Almost all high-ranking secret police officials from across the country were summoned to Moscow, never to be seen again. JJeswiped out Soviet military intelligence. The legendary old man alias General Grisham alias Yan Berzon, the director of the Red Army Intelligence Administration, was recalled from Spain and executed in 1937. At the same time, the NKVD killed scores of its agents. Unidentified bodies have been discovered in the dark alleyways of Paris, Geneva, and other cities. Terror seized the Red Army High Command in June 1937. Tukacevski, Lubavitch, Idaman, Koch, and other enlightened high-ranking officers were charged with anti-Soviet treason and executed.

Less than a year later, the officers who tried Tukhachevsky and his colleagues were fired. Air Force Supreme Commander Yakov Alexknis, Far Eastern Army Commander Vasily Bucha, Leningrad Military District Commander Pavel Dubenko, and Marshall Alexander Yogorov were all killed, along with tens of thousands of officers of various ranks and positions. This purge's accomplishment was celebrated in a meeting commemorating the 20th anniversary of the Soviet security establishment, beginning with the Cheka, then the OGPU, and now the NKVD.

The gathering took place on December 20th, 1937, at the Bolshoi Theatre. "Every citizen of the USSR is an employee of the NKVD," Enestas McCoyyan declared. The anniversary was observed across the country. Yossef received the Order of Lenin. His name was given to military units, economic enterprises, and even machines. Yossef, who was committed to Stalin, increased his efforts. The purges of 1937-38 targeted Stalin's most ardent followers, including Commissar of Justice Nikolai Kirilenko and former Cheka officer Yosef Unslict. Vladimir Antonov, one of the heroes of the October Revolution, was recalled from his diplomatic post and shot, as was would-be former NKVD chairman Yagoda.

Yagoda was the main witness and collaborator in Stalin's crimes, including Kirov's murder. When Stalin was unable to evade public suspicions about the execution, he blamed the NKVD, commanded by Yagoda. Yagoda was suddenly linked to Trotsky and blamed for the deaths of Mendzinsky and Gorky. Yagoda was named as one of the main defendants in the third Moscow trial. Along with him were Nikolai Bukharin, a politburo member and theoretician, Alexei Rakov, the Soviet government's head, Nikolai Christines, Lenin's former deputy, and Christian Rockoffski, the respective Bolshevik and Soviet Ukraine's leader. The prosecutor was the infamous Andrei Wyszynski. "Bukharin and Rakov, along with their associates, systematically provided information to various foreign intelligence services." Spies from Germany and Poland buzzed over Yagoda like insects. He not only protected them, but he also spied for them." As a prosecutor, Wyszynski was more concerned with confessions than with factual evidence.

The NKVD would compel confessions. Its agents used the most heinous tortures without authorization. The only option to avoid torture was to commit suicide, and some dared to do so, including Micahel Tomsky, Yaya Manik, and Fiats Cryptic. Buherron Rieckhoff and the other defendants in the third Moscow trial would do whatever to be shot as citizens' enemies. In the Soviet regime, which deliberately killed the old Bolsheviks and waged war on ordinary people, justice vanished. The future of everyone was unknown. The NKVD has the authority to arrest anyone, at anytime, anywhere. Everyone beyond the age of 12 was subject to criminal liability and penalties under a 1935 law. Children may be imprisoned or sentenced to death. The atrocities of Yossef's torment were condemned in the West, and Roland opposed child detention.

Stalin's rule was labeled fascist by Andre Gide. Even Herbert Wells, who had always supported the Soviet cause, could no longer offer positive remarks. Stalin, though, had allies. When Leon Feuchtwanger visited the Soviet Union in 1937, he composed an ode to Stalin. "My initial impression is that Stalin is very unpretentious, and the Soviet people respect and love him." No one is more deserving of representing 170 million people."

Feuchtwanger was among those who saw socialism as a panacea for modern-day evils. He favored Stalin over Hitler. Stalin was now the absolute ruler of Russia. Terror became a typical technique of state governance for him. Stalin required new executioners because it was time to kill the witnesses to his most recent atrocities. Lavrentiy Beria was appointed as Yossef's deputy on July 28, 1938. Unlike Stalin's previous protégées, Beria was a professional secret police officer as well as a party apparatchik. Beria's guile, insidiousness, and remarkable energy helped him to quickly establish a career in the Georgian Cheka in his early twenties. He was only 30 years old when he was appointed chairman.

He was appointed OGPU plenipotentiary for the whole Transcaucasia in 1929. Stalin got aware of him while on vacation in Georgia. Beria rose the ranks and is currently at the top of the party's leadership. In 1931, he was appointed the party's first secretary in Georgia, and within a few years, he had established, in Stalin's opinion, the Republic's rightful order Beria became Georgia's dictator in 1937, a smaller-scale Stalin. He annihilated all his opponents, including Stalin's favorite Nestola Cobra, the head of Abkhazian autonomy. Likova was chosen as Yagoda's successor at the NKVD, but he declined the position.

He would not abandon hazy, instead competing for dominance in Transcaucasia with ba carrier. Beria poisoned Likova over dinner in 1936. A year later, all of Likova's relatives were exterminated. Beria arrived in Moscow without hesitation when Stalin summoned him. He took charge immediately after being appointed as Yusuf's deputy. His appointment as chief of the NKVD was announced in the press on December 9th, 1938. Yossef, like his predecessor Yagoda, was condemned and disappeared. The same magnificent Sons of the Motherland who had lately been recognized by the Kremlin, as well as the NKVD officers who had carried out his commands. Beria hinted at a more fafavorableolitical situation. Several dozen gulag inmates were released, including Constantine Raucousofski, Andre Tupolev, and Lev Landau, but other inmates replaced them. Among Stalin's victims was his recent favorite Komsomol leader Alexander KKosovo "There is nothing more significant in life for Soviet youngsters than our great Bolshevik Communist Party and our dear beloved Comrade Stalin." Komsomol, the epitome of loyalty, was abruptly chastised for failing to aid the NKVD in exposing foes. Beria personally detained him in his home in November 1938. Komsomol was executed three months later.

Among the victims were Theater Director for Cephalon Mayor Holt, who was accused of supporting Trotsky and espionage for four other countries. He was never released from prison. His wife, actress Ida Reich, was stabbed to death by NKVD assassins. Mikhail Koltsov, a journalist, and Isaac Babble, a writer, were both shots after being accused of anti-Soviet Pro Trotsky activities. Before their execution, the NKVD interviewed them to obtain evidence against other notable intellectuals. The secret police planned another sham trial for writers Maurice Pasternak, Ilya Ehrenburg, and composer Dmitri Shostakovich. The warmer political climate in Baria did not prevent detainees from being tortured. Baria took part in person.

Bread trucks secretly transported the bodies of those who perished to the cremation, and their ashes were scattered in the fields of a collective farm near Moscow. In 1940, Baria oversaw the assassination of Trotsky, Stalin's most despised foe. The NKVD hired Rehman Masada, who attacked Trotsky with an ice axe in his Mexico City study. On August 21st, Trotsky passed away. Masada was awarded the golden star of Hero of the Soviet Union after serving 20 years in a Mexican prison. In 1978, he died in Cuba and was buried in Moscow as Rahman Ivanovich Lopez. The NKVD began purging the newly conquered Baltic states of Estonia, Latvia, and Lithuania in August 1940. Those accused of anti-Soviet views were exiled in October. Others followed in 1941 and 1944, totaling over 700,000 individuals.

The Soviet Union was on the verge of war. Military intelligence was Semyon Timoshenko's domain, but it was Baria who had the most up-to-date knowledge on the approaching Nazi assault. He and Stalin are both to blame for the 1941 military disaster. Stalin refused to admit Hitler's invasion intentions, and Baria purposefully suppressed accumulating evidence. Even before the Nazi onslaught, Baria protested to Stalin that spies were attempting to create fear. The war increased the NKVD's workload but did not affect their techniques. Trains began transporting more inmates to the gulag almost immediately after the conflict began. Their offenses varied, such as spreading stories or causing fear. Failure to surrender radio receivers and radio paths, as well as soldiers who had survived encirclement, people from captured territories, and German prisoners of war. Entire ethnic groups throughout the United States were massacred in 1943. Russia was suspected of working with the Germans.

Russian Germans, Kalmyks, Chechens, and others were relocated. Siberia, Kazakhstan, and the far north's wilderness in 1944 were followed by the Crimean Tatars. The NKVD organized SMERSH killing squadrons just behind the front lines, with limitless permission to execute traitors, deserters, and anyone who retreated. The NKVD also had fighting troops and sabotage battalions that operated behind enemy lines. The NKVD directed resistance and guerrilla movement units in enemy-controlled territory The Germans discovered the mass burial of Polish officers in the Katene woodland near Smolensk in 1943. The NKVD was charged. Following the liberation of Smolensk, Beria created a Board of Investigation to determine whether the people were executed by the Germans, even if it meant suppressing evidence. The Western Allies wanted to maintain their ties with the Soviet Union at the time, therefore they avoided the issue.

Only recently did records from the NKVD archives establish beyond doubt that the Polish officers were assassinated on Baria's direct order in 1940. He also ordered the death of Polish inmates in camps near Kalinin and Kharkiv, killing around 22,000 Polish officers in all. There were about two million German POWs in Russia when the war came to a close. The NKVD was forced to use this workforce, but it was only a fraction of the slave laborers engaged in the most critical and demanding building projects - the majority of whom were Soviet criminals. Their number was steadily growing.

Returnees from German POW camps were incarcerated in the gulag. Stalin congratulated Baria and his officers. Baria received the Lenin and red banner orders here. He won the Order of Suvarov, the highest medal for a military commander, for his work in resettling the North Caucasian and Crimean nations. He was also named a socialist labor hero. Shortly after the war, Baria, who had only seen action twice, was appointed Marshal of the Soviet Union. He accompanied Stalin to the Potsdam Conference and was tasked with inspecting defeated Germany's factories. Stalin kept promoting him. Baria focussed on his duties in the Politburo and the Foreign Ministry in 1946. At the same time, as head of the Ministry of State Security, he was tasked with overseeing nuclear research. Terror was maintained by Baria's devoted followers, Deccan Asaf, Gog Leeds, and Merkulov.

Another purge was planned, to destroy the Jewish anti-fascist committee. Following the Nazi invasion, Stalin convened a meeting of Jewish representatives in Moscow. Salomon Michals, Ilya Ehrenberg, and other notable Jewish thinkers had appealed to brethren all over the world to aid the Soviet Union combat Nazism. Their case was heard.

The Jewish Council for Aid to Russia was established in the United States and is led by Einstein, Albert. The committee became obsolete after the war. In January 1948, its chairman, Solomon Michaels, is dispatched to Minsk with an NKVD art specialist to examine Theater performances. Michaels never returned from the trip; he was killed in an automobile accident. Many other committee members were imprisoned, and some died during the three years of interrogation that followed, while the others were executed in 1952. Barbara planned to broaden his power base in his late 40s. Gyorgi Malenkov, Stalin's closest supporter, fell out of favor and lost his job as Central Committee secretary, making the task even more difficult. This elevated Andrey Zhdanov, a prominent opponent, and his faction to significant posts. However, Zhdanov died unexpectedly in 1948, and Malenkov regained his previous role. Barnier and Malenkov could control all other party officials and thus the entire country if they worked together. Only Stalin wielded more power, but on March 1, 1953, Stalin suffered a stroke and died soon after.

On March 9, Baria delivered a eulogy from the Lenin mausoleum, hinting that he would be the future party head. Baria attempted to consolidate authority by appointing Malenkov as co-chairman of the Council of Ministers. State security forces were integrated with police under the Ministry of Home Affairs, led by Baria, at Malenkov's request. Baria planned to assassinate his party's elite opponents, Molotov, Sheganovich, Buganon, and Khrushchev and discreetly set his soldiers on high alert. The strategy failed. Sergei Lavrov and Evan Serif, his deputies, betrayed him and alerted Nikita Khrushchev of the imminent coup. Khrushchev overcame the obstacle and rapidly gained the approval of all the central committee officials.

Malenkov, in particular, and Defense Minister Deputy Yogi Zhukov. On June 26th, 1953, Baria was detained in the Kremlin on Khrushchev's orders. He was executed six months later. Three months later, Khrushchev appointed Yvonne Serov as the inaugural chairman of a new institution that would come to be known as the KGB, the State Security Committee. The Soviet Security Service would continue to operate under its new name for nearly four decades, following in the footsteps of the Cheka, OGPU, and NKVD.

Chapter Five

How Stalin's Nkvd Spies Took Down Trotsky

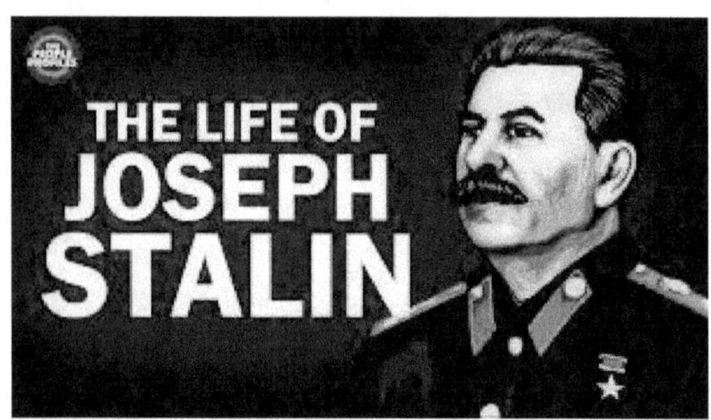

Joseph Stalin was the most powerful and ruthless dictator in modern history – for decades until he died in 1953, he ruled the largest country in the world the Soviet Union with an iron fist. He based his absolute power and his secret police the NKVD then the largest intelligence service in the world his agents were highly professional and unspeakably brutal. The NKVD's primary mission was to serve Stalin and destroy his enemies both at home and abroad. The might of the NKVD was deeply rooted in a common turn an international communist organization headquartered in Moscow. By the middle of the 1930s the Comintern united over 60 communist parties around the world. The Comintern had its intelligence department.

On orders from the Soviet leadership, communists began spying in their own countries. The Soviet spy apparatus in the 30s and 40s had an international flavor to it, so they would very carefully try to see if they couldn't get some people to do some things for them under the guise of you are cooperating with the worldwide communist movement.

This is for a better future and the world. Delegates from around the world regularly came to Moscow to attend Comintern congresses. Here they received their marching orders in the fight for global dominance. Fanatically devoted to communist ideas, many of them would become Soviet spies - some would become assassins. Soviet intelligence - the NKVD in the middle of the 1930s had two priorities. One is very difficult in the West for us at all to understand, and the priority was who killed Stalin's opponents outside the Soviet Union; simply to kill Trotsky and the leading Trotskyists.

The other priority which is easier for us to understand was to collect intelligence about the West. Leon Trotsky was Stalin's greatest enemy. He was everything Stalin wasn't; a prodigious intellect, a charismatic organizer of the Russian October Revolution in 1917, and the founder of the Red Army. Trotsky had loyal supporters around the world who called themselves Trotskyists. Many Russians believed Trotsky would succeed Lenin as the head of the new red Empire, but Stalin had other plans. He knew how to work the levers of power through backroom intrigues, blackmail, and terror. Within five years of Lenin's death, Trotsky was stripped of all political offices exiled and branded a traitor, an enemy of the people. But Leon Trotsky didn't give up.

From Mexico, he organized an international campaign to fight Stalinism. In 1936, Spain erupted into civil war. The red-wing nationalists of General Francisco Franco led a coup against the socialist Republican government. Adolf Hitler rushed to General Franco's aid, sending weapons and military advisors. The Socialists formed a left-wing coalition with Trotskyists and communists. Stalin supported the left in strengthening the communist movement in Europe, as well as heavy artillery, planes, and military advisors he sent secret agents and experts in guerrilla warfare and terrorism. The NKVD succeeded in infiltrating the socialist

Republican government. This allowed them to launch their secret war, taking the Spanish secret services under full control. The NKVD was to help the republican government defeat General Franco, but the desire to help the left against the right in the Spanish Civil War was quickly overtaken by Stalin's traditional obsessions. Stalin ordered the NKVD to make its main appellate, not the Nationalists, but the Trotskyists within the republican movement. Communist volunteers from France, Britain, the United States, and Germany flocked to Spain.

Together with Spanish socialists, they formed International Brigades. After a quick course in warfare taught by Soviet military experts, they were armed and ready to go into battle - unaware of the danger posed by NKVD agents.French agitator Andrey Mati also came to Spain ostensibly to represent comment on the International communist organization, but he was also an NKVD agent with a secret mission to kill Trotsky's supporters. He signed the execution warrants for over 500 interbred members, suspected of Trotskyism. American writer and journalist Ernest Hemingway then wrote about him "He is as crazy as a bedbug. He has a mania for shooting people" The NKVD also made use of the passports held by communist volunteers. On the way to Spain, volunteers first had to go through a reception center in France. It was controlled by NKVD agents who took passports from all the newcomers to keep them safe as they put it. They sent the most suitable passports to Moscow to the Secret Service headquarters with the pictures changed. Soviet agents would use these passports on their secret missions around the world.

While thousands died for freedom and democracy on the battlefields of Spain, Stalin hatched another plot. He ordered the NKVD spymaster in Spain Alexander All off to find a way to secure Spain's gold reserves and bring them to Moscow without leaving any written receipts of the transaction. Acting through leading Spanish communists all off persuaded the Spanish republican government to send the gold to Moscow for safekeeping.

The golden nuggets then valued at 500 million dollars were loaded onto a Soviet steamer and sent to Moscow. Years later, Franco's government repeatedly petitioned Soviet leaders to return the gold. Each time the Russians refused - claiming that during the Civil War, the Spanish socialist government spent all the money on weapons used to fight General Franco.

Meanwhile, the war in Spain dragged on. Elsewhere in Europe, a wave of mysterious political killings swept through the land. People who had been defined by Joseph Stalin and by the intelligence leadership as enemies of the people were killed by so-called mobile groups who wandered around Europe, largely under false identities, searching out opportunities and techniques for killing people. Lausanne, Switzerland, on the 4th of September 1937 three men entered a cafe and requested permission to join a man sitting alone at one of the tables. The man was Dignity Rice, a disillusioned NKVD agent who had broken ties with a Secret Service and had become an outspoken critic of Stalin. After a while, all four men stood up and left. In the street, they stepped into a car. The next day, the dead body of Dignity Rice was found on a country road outside of Lausanne, riddled with bullets. The Bolshevik Revolution made three million Russians flee the country, among them were officers and soldiers of the Russian Tzars army. They formed an opposition group called the white movement the Bolsheviks considered the white movement dangerous to their regime and planned a series of terrorist acts against its leaders.

Generally, Evgeny Miller became one of the targets. Paris, France, on the 22nd of September in 1937, two NKVD agents and French police uniforms approached generally Afghani Miller in the street. They pushed him into a car and sped off. General Miller was drugged and brought to Moscow by ship. He was tortured and then executed without a trial. Ukrainian nationalists were also on the list of Stalin's enemies. They had never accepted the Soviet regime in Ukraine. Their leader in exile colonel Afghani Konevalitz lived in Rotterdam, Holland. In the twenties, Konevalitz fought against Russian communists for an independent Ukraine - known for his tireless hatred of communists Konevalitz continued his fight against

Holland. Stalin gave a special mission to one of his best agents Pavel Sudoplatov. Sudoplatov was to pose as a nephew of one of Konevalitz's friends who died recently.

Sudoplatov explained: "Stalin listen to my report and Konevalitz's and said he likes chocolates - doesn't he? Well, let's give him some chocolates." NKVD experts made a special box of chocolates with a miniature but powerful time bomb set to explode a few minutes after delivery. The explosive was hidden under a layer of real chocolates.

Sudoplatov arrived in Holland aboard a Soviet ship carrying two boxes of chocolates; one harmless and another that was charged. He made plans to meet Colonel Konevalitz in Rotterdam at a small downtown restaurant. Sudoplatov explained: "We gave him both boxes as a present from Ukraine and he said in Ukrainian - thank you
My friend, and put both boxes into his pockets. We talked a little, then I excused myself and left. I was in a small shop nearby when I heard the explosion. I didn't go back to look. I couldn't do anything more anyway."

The explosion tore Colonel Connor's valance to pieces. In the late 1930s, Stalin continued his fierce fight against his enemies both real and imagined. Inside the country he launched mass repression against his people - no suspects were spared including his secret police. Abroad, his number-one enemy Leon Trotsky was still alive. Trotsky said: "The general has ceased to be the center of the world. It is foolish to hope that Europe will again occupy that position.

The present terrific crisis despite its devastating effects on the United States will change the relation of forces. Still further, not in favor of Europe with in favor of the United States in the colonial countries." Moscow 1937, the Bolshoi Theatre, Nikolai Jakov, head of the NKVD presided over the 20th anniversary of the celebration of the establishment of the Secret police. "Glory to NKVD, glory to Conrad Basil who teaches us to work in comrade Stalin's way." Nikolai Azov was a sadist and a willing executioner for Josef Stalin. By now Stalin growing increasingly paranoid had launched an era of unprecedented repressions and terror, known as the Great Purges. Mass murder became institutionalized in the Soviet Union - millions were arrested and executed as enemies of the people. Stalin's secret police were put in charge of the purges and loyally served their master, but no one was safe - not even Stalin's most feared accomplices – were the agents in the NKVD. What were the reasons for Stalin's purges in the intelligence service?

First, Stalin did not trust anybody who had ever been abroad. In his opinion, they could have been re-recruited. Second, many agents were close to Trotskyism and other ideas opposing Stalin's policy. This was much worse than being suspected as a double agent. Even Stalin's loyal executioner Nikolay Gearsoff was arrested. An executioner came straight after two years of the cell to kill him.

An experienced master of martial arts years off kept running around the cell dodging bullets the gunman had to empty his pistol before he hit Gearsoff. The new head of Stalin's secret police was Lavrentiy Beria, Gearsoff equal was a sadist and murderer. Stalin entrusted him with a mission he'd been cherishing for over 15 years - the assassination of Leon Trotsky. Trotsky had become in Stalin'simagination the devil incarnates - a true Antichrist

Trotsky hoped that he was beyond Stalin's reach at a lonely heavily guarded villa near Mexico City. MJVD chief Lavrentiy Beria took one of his best agents Pavel Sudoplatov to meet Stalin. Sudoplatov explained: "He came into Stalin's office and he asked; are you ready to operate? I answered I'm sorry cannot perform it personally as I've never been to Mexico and I don't speak Spanish. But I suggested he assigned this mission to my deputy Nam Haeseong - an experienced and highly qualified agent.

Stalin said take Haeseong, take whomever you want, and start." Haeseong was an NKVD veteran of the Spanish Civil War and a wily recruiter for his agency. He had brought Mexico's foremost painter Dahveedsee Karros one of the founders of the Mexican Communist Party into his fold. In time, Haeseong developed two plans to kill Trotsky. On the night of the 23rd of May 1940, Karros and 20 hit men armed with submachine guns burst into Trotsky's villa and sprayed his bedroom with bullets.

But Trotsky and his wife managed to throw themselves under the bed. The police subsequently accounted for 70 bullet holes in his bedroom wall but not one of those bullets hit Trotsky. Haeseong had a lover of Spanish communists; Caridad Mercado. Together with her son Ramon the threesome launched a standby operation posing as a Trotskyist, Ramon Mercado seduced Trotsky's secretary. Soon he was a frequent visitor to Trotsky's Villa and a familiar face to his security guards. By the 20th of August 1940, Ramon was ready.

He drove to Trotsky's villa with his mother and the meeting was on. Inside the premises, Mercado played shy. He asked Trotsky to have a look at an article that he'd written on Trotskyism.

Trotsky took him up to his study, and started reading the article, while he was reading the article Ramon took out from his pocket an ice pick, lifted it in his two hands, and brought it down on the back of Trotsky's head. Trotsky left out a terrible scream. Trotsky's security men ran into the study and grabbed Ramon Mercado. When his mother now mating gone saw police cars arriving at the villa, they hastily beat a retreat. Leon Trotsky was taken to a nearby hospital. He suffered horribly through the night and died the next day. From an export company's office building in New York, now Haeseong masterminded Trotsky's assassination. Soviet intelligence agents had also used this company and many others like it as a front for their communication centers abroad. From the early 1930s when they began setting up their spy network on the American continent, Soviet intelligence agents were making themselves very comfortable in the United States.

Soviet spies had been operating in North America long before the Second World War. They were researching for information related to American foreign policy, economic developments, and military potential. Later, during the war, the Soviets used this knowledge to build their relationship with the United States. They decided that a good recruitment pool for spies and spying in the United States was the commie's party. If you look at the American Communist Party in the 30s and 40s, there was no reason to not like the Soviet Union. They represented tomorrow in a way. Soviet intelligence had a well-developed spy network at all levels of President Roosevelt's administration; journalist Whitaker Chambers served as the main link between them and Moscow. His contacts included Alger Hiss at the Ministry of Agriculture, Gary White at the Ministry of Finance, and others. In the 1930s over 50 official's summit very senior levels cooperated with Soviet intelligence. If you happen to be working for the United States government at that time and you were in the Communist Party at that time and you had been recruited by one of the Soviet recruiters, the line would be "help us help the world". The Soviets received a treasure trove of secret scientific economic and military information, not only on the United States but also on Germany, Britain, and other countries. The secret information files and rolls of microfilm were passed to Soviet handlers through two key couriers; Whittaker Chambers and Elizabeth Bentley.

American and British security in the mid-1930s was so absurdly weak that collecting British secrets and collecting American secrets has never been easier. For years, the Soviet spying operation gathered intelligence. Then in 1939, a series of shocking events made many Americans cooperating with the NKVD completely changed their views of the Soviet Union. On the 23rd of August, theNazi Minister of Foreign Affairs Yokeem von Ribbentrop flew to Moscow. His visit had been arranged in such haste that Soviet anti-aircraft units had not been notified, and a few shots were fired at the Ribbentrop plane as if it were an enemy aircraft. Later that day, the unthinkable happened. Soviet Russia signed a non-aggression pact with its archrival Nazi Germany.

Then they signed a friendship pact. The pact had several secret appendices with plans to divide a conquered Europe between Germany and the Soviet Union. The Soviet-Nazi pact sealed the fate of Europe. Within days of the 1st of September Germany invaded Poland from the west. Two weeks later, Stalin joined from the east. The world was at war. By 1939, Whittaker Chambers had become disillusioned with the communist ideals and had been avoiding his Soviet handlers for nearly a year, but he kept silent until September 2nd, 1939.

The Soviet-Nazi pact so incensed Chambers that with no fear of the consequences, he revealed his spying activities to President Roosevelt's advisor Adolf Berle Jr. Burrell immediately sent an urgent report on Soviet espionage to President Roosevelt, titled "Underground EspionageAgent." Roosevelt ignored the report. He underestimated the potential the Soviet intelligence in the US and refused to believe that the Soviets had so thoroughly infiltrated his administration. The signing of the non-aggression pact and the friendship treaty with Germany marked one of the most dramatic moments in the history of Soviet intelligence. Within hours, it seemed Germany had turned from enemy number one into the closest friend and ally. Stalin ordered intelligence activities inside Hitler's Germany cut down, and phraseology to cut down meant to ban it almost completely.

Stalin's behavior during the last months before Hitler's invasion remains a mystery. Some historians claim that he trusted Hitler, or he believed that Hitler would follow conventional military wisdom, and not fight on two fronts at the same time. It meant that he wouldn't attack the Soviet Union before the end of the war with Great Britain. With Hitler tied up in a war against Britain, Stalin saw his opportunity.

At a secret meeting with his closest aides, he declared that communism would need a global war to conquer the world. Stalin said that the Soviet Union should help Hitler to fight against Britain and France to make the US join the war to save Britain. According to Stalin, the Soviet Union would wait till the capitalists weakened each other and then deliver a crucial strike from the east to liberate Europe. Part of Stalin planned to strike Nazi Germany when Hitler's army was heavily engaged in Western Europe. Perhaps Stalin's order to cut down spying activities and Nazi Germany was simply to help maintain his appearance as friendship. He did not want to alert Hitler to his intentions. Stalin refused to revise his plans even after receiving crucial intelligence about Hitler's preparations for an invasion of the Soviet Union. Several sources were warning them of a coming German invasion.

They were receiving information from practically all over Europe and even from the United States, but the key information came from the Red Orchestra. The Red Orchestra was the largest intelligence network of the war. Under the leadership of Leopold Trapper, one of the brightest agents in Soviet military intelligence, the Red Orchestra had agents all over Europe and they were getting very disturbing news. Just before the war, Leopold Trapper set up a company in Paris. It successfully traded in construction materials and remained in business even after the Nazis occupied Paris.

The company was a front for Trevor's real job as a Soviet military spymaster. By the spring of 1940, Trapper controlled 7 major intelligent networks with over 200 active agents based in France, Holland, Belgium, and Germany. Throughout the fall of 1940, the battle for Britain raged on. In the first stage of Germany's operation Sea Lion which called for the eventual invasion of Britain, Luftwaffe bombers rained terror on British cities including the devastating non-stop bombing of London. The world waited for the invasion of the Beleaguered Island. German paratroopers were still on invasion alert when Leopold Trooper sent an urgent coded message to Moscow. Hitler had canceled his plans for the invasion - something was afoot. Soon after, three German divisions stationed on the Atlantic coast were transferred to the Polish town of Poznan - close to the Soviet border. On the 18th of December 1940, Hitler signed directive Number 21 - Operation Barbarossa, his plan to invade the Soviet Union. Less than two weeks later, Stalin received information about Barbarossa from his agents in Europe. Soon after the intelligence was confirmed by Stalin's key spy in Japan: Richard Sergei. Sergei was among the most clever and fearless spies of World War two. The information he sent back to Russia was priceless and instrumental in changing the outcome of the war.

Richard Sergei was born in Russia to a German father and a Russian mother. As a kid went to Germany and served in the German army in World War I. In 1920, he gets enamored with the communist party, building the new Russia and building the new world. He begins to work for Russian military intelligence. In 1933 Sergei went to Germany on a secret mission. He joined the Nazi Party and started working for one of the major German daily newspapers; the Frankfurter Zeitung. Shortly thereafter, he was sent to Japan as the paper's Asian correspondent. In Tokyo, representing a German newspaper and letting out very Pro-Nazi views and feelings to whomever he meets, he gets along beautifully with the Japanese, who are fascists and he's a hero to them. He's a German and he is Nazism was personified in his political views, so a lot of Japanese politicians and even some military share their views with him, which Sergei immediately sends back to Russia. In Tokyo, Richard Sergei began a frequent and welcome visitor at the German Embassy. In 1939, the German ambassador to Japan General Ogun Otto appointed Sergei the official press attache of the embassy.

The two men became close friends. By that time, Sergei had a well-functioning operation. His agents infiltrated the highest echelon of military and political power in Japan. Miles away in Siberia, secret Soviet radio stations regularly received transmissions containing top-secret information about military preparations both in Japan and Germany, signed by Sergei's codename Brahms. One of his cables contained key excerpts from the top-secret operation Barbarossa. It read; "The Armed Forces of Vermacht must be ready to destroy Soviet Russia in a Blitzkrieg Campaign before the end of the war against Great Britain." Barbarossa was a top-secret plan. Only eight people knew about it in Germany. A few weeks later the plan was on Stalin's table, but Stalin did not believe in his intelligence. He could not acknowledge that his intelligence service was so brilliant that it managed to get this information so quickly. When Stalin learned Sergei was the source, his only remark was "it's a provocation - he's a double agent". Sergei's fate was sealed. He was ominously summoned to Moscow, but Sergei did not obey. He decided not to return. Meanwhile, Stalin's agents in other countries were warning of a coming invasion. In Geneva, Switzerland Hungarian scientist Sandor Rado had established a highly successful cartographic company.

His reputation was so good that he received orders for large-scale maps of different European regions from the German military. Unknown to them, Sandor Rado was also a spy. The head of one of the largest Soviet intelligence networks in Switzerland and Germany. He operated under the codename; Dora. Two weeks before Hitler's invasion of Larhonda transmitted a very important covert communication to the Soviet Union. "To start, all German motorized divisions previously stationed along the Swiss border have been relocated to the southeast." Germany now has 150 divisions on its eastern border. Preparations are far more intense than they were in April and May.

Dora, please sign." Sandor Rado sent another telegram from Switzerland a few days before the invasion. "Ursula Kuczynski, codenamed Sonya, was one of Rado's top female spies."

During this time in Switzerland, I was responsible for training three radio operators for Sandor Rado. I'm not sure which of them it was. Perhaps it was my husband who relayed Rado's message to Moscow. It was a coded message, and the radio operator had no idea what it said. The letter alerted Moscow that the war would commence on June 22nd, with German soldiers relocating. Your source is untrustworthy, according to the response. Rado was desperate now." Any information that did not correspond to Stalin's strategy was either a lie, a mistake, or a provocation.

The new NKVD chief, Pavel Hedden, proceeded to double-check the veracity of these worrisome reports. He dispatched a lovely lady, an experienced agent named Zoya Rybkina, to a reception at the German Embassy in Moscow. "When I arrived at the embassy, German ambassador Count Schulenburg invited me to a tangle. Schulenburg appeared to be melancholy. I inquired, "Count, are you in a terrible mood?" He responded, "Oh no, who could be in a foul mood in excellent company as you?" When I looked at the walls, I noticed light spots on the wallpaper where photos had been removed. Then I noticed numerous packed luggage through a half-open door to one of the rooms. I asked him again, "Are you still alive?" German embassies from Moscow to Tokyo were humming with activity by this point. Sergei reported to Moscow from Japan, and the German ambassador in Tokyo, General Otto, received confirmation from von Ribbentrop that Germany would invade in the second half of June.

This information is without a doubt correct. He sent another cable a few days later. The warning was succinct: "The war will begin on June 22nd, 1941." "We question your validity," Moscow responded, Information." Sergei was desperate now, insisting that the fate of millions was at stake. He sent Stalin yet another cable. It contained his most ominous message. "I repeat, nine armies with 150 divisions will cross the border and assault the Soviet Union." On the 22nd of June."

Hitler's army attacked on June 22, 1941. The strike was terrible. The German Blitzkrieg destroyed nearly all of the Russian tanks, artillery pieces, and aircraft stationed near the border on the first day. Most Soviet planes never took off from their runways. The Germans killed practically the entire Red Army over the next four months, killing three and a half million soldiers. Another 1.5 million soldiers were taken, prisoner. Only then did Stalin appeal to his spymasters for assistance, and he had one very important question for them. Hitler's army was closing in on Moscow by the end of October 1941. Fear of a Japanese attack in Siberia weakened Stalin'sdefensess even further.

Army units that were desperately needed to protect Moscow were stationed in the Far East in preparation for a possible Japanese onslaught. The Japanese were still debating whether to attack the Soviets in Siberia or the British and Americans in Southeast Asia. The most important Soviet spy in Japan Sergei had numerous operatives and connections in the Japanese government. For months, he'd been attempting to persuade them that the Japanese would be far better off acquiring valuable resources such as tin, rubber, and oil in Southeast Asia than facing a grueling winter war in Siberia. Sergei eventually discovered that Japan had abandoned its plans to attack the Soviet Union. Stalin had been anticipating this news. Sergei had Moscow's ear after properly forecasting the German attack. Sergei had purchased a fishing boat months before, and he and his radio operator had installed a radio transmitter and began making regular boat journeys into the open sea to broadcast radio signals. Sergei took the boat out alone on a day when his operator was unwell and communicated important information.

The most essential information he conveyed back to Moscow is that he can advise Stalin that the Japanese had no intention of entering Siberia to support the Germans, and Stalin can take advantage of this intelligence.

Many of the divisions he had in Siberia to combat the Japanese were transferred to his Western Front. It saved Moscow, the Russian capital, at the last minute. On the 24th anniversary of the Bolshevik Revolution, November 7, 1941, new Russian troops from Siberia paraded through Moscow. They marched straight from the parade to the front lines, only 40 kilometers from Red Square. The German offensive came to a standstill outside of Moscow. It was their first defeat in World War II. Sergei's biggest victory was also his final.

He was unmasked and imprisoned by Japanese military intelligence after eight years undercover. Sergei was one of a small group of determined, inventive, and daring Soviet intelligence agents who made a significant contribution to Russia's war effort. In an operation codenamed Monastery, the Soviets succeeded to plant one of their best men in a critical German post early in 1942. Alexandra Demyanov was an experienced NKVD agent. He reached the front line in February 1942 and persuaded the Germans that he was committed to their cause. The Germans sent him to their military intelligence school to be educated.

Demyanov was given the pseudonym Max after completing the course and was sent back to Moscow to coordinate Nazi spying and espionage. Demyanov was to meet with terrorists brought to Russia by Germans and assist them in organizing sabotage missions. As a result of his operations, the NKVD apprehended and executed some of the terrorists. Demyanov alone assisted the NKVD in neutralizing nearly 50 German agents in Moscow. Demyanov was assigned to General Rokossovsky's headquarters as a communications officer by the NKVD.

Demyanov provided the Germans with misinformation regularly, mixed with just enough accurate intelligence to keep them from uncovering the truth, even if it meant sacrificing Russian blood. In early November 1942, for example, Max sent a wire to his German employers stating, "The Red Army will deliver strikes in the Northern Caucasus and at Reshef on November 15th." This was correct information. Even though the best Soviet general, Georgy Zhukov, was in charge of the preparations, the Germans, who had been warned by Demyanov, successfully repelled the onslaught.

Zhukov himself had no idea what was going on behind his unsuccessful advance as a man at the age of four. The Soviet attack was a ruse devised by Stalin and his close advisers to divert German soldiers away from Stalingrad, a crucial strategic supply center. The siege of Stalingrad had lasted six months, with a fierce fight for every inch of soil and every house. The main Soviet force launched a strong onslaught against the German army once the reserve fainted. The Germans were dealt their second crushing loss of the war. 300,000 men were imprisoned, and thousands more perished. Hitler's Blitzkrieg came to a stop at Stalingrad. It was also a pivotal moment in the fight. Alexander Demyanov, a double spy, was the only person honored by both sides for the same operation. The Germans awarded him the Military Cross with Swords, while the Russians awarded him the Red Star. Nicolay Kuznetsov, another Russian agent, freely mixed with Nazis in the controlled countries. Nicolay Kuznetsov was a remarkable individual; image learning the German language nearly entirely by himself as a young man from a Siberian village. Germans can tell where someone is from based on their dialect. Kuznetsov spoke seven or eight dialects of German. Kuznetsov was a member of a partisan group at the time.

Vinnytsia is a Ukrainian town. From there, he conducted attacks on German-occupied territory while impersonating a German officer named Poles Ebert. This was a heavily guarded zone, which Hitler himself visited. Kuznetsov informed Moscow one day that a well-known German espionage master named Otto Skorzeny was training a group of terrorists in Vinnytsia for a unique covert mission. Kuznetsov grew close to one of Skorzeny's officers. The cop was dating one of Kuznetsov's agents. The officer informed the girl that he was departing shortly and promised to bring her a Persian rug as a gift.

The girl didn't take it seriously, but like a good agent, she informed Kuznetsov about the chat. He notified Moscow, which was the missing connection. For leads, Soviet intelligence personnel sought Persia or Iran. They concluded that an assassination attempt would be attempted in Tehran, where the three allied leaders, Stalin, Roosevelt, and Churchill, were scheduled to meet to address a critical issue: the beginning of the second European front the Soviets dispatched.

To prevent the effort, extra army units and a powerful anti-terrorist NKVD group were deployed. As a precaution, Stalin offered President Roosevelt to stay in the Soviet mansion when he arrived in Tehran. Roosevelt graciously accepted the invitation. The NKVD unit liquidated a German terrorist squad in Tehran on December 2nd, 1943, at 6 a.m. If Stalin had listened to his operatives, the Russian victory would have come much sooner and with far less loss of life, but he never admitted to any mistakes. In 1944, he delivered a speech to party members commemorating the 27th anniversary of the Bolshevik Revolution. "History demonstrates that aggressive nations who are ready to fight are usually better equipped for a new war than defensive nations," he said. Nations that value peace there is no question that peace-loving nations will be caught off guard in the future." Even though Stalin offered

According to this argument, he was attempting to destroy the few persons who recognized the true cost the country had to pay for the suspicion of his intelligence service. Fearing Stalin's purges, Alexander Orloff escaped to the United States. He spent the rest of his life terrified of the NKVD's retaliation. Leopold Tripper, the head of the Red Orchestra who delivered the news of the impending Nazi invasion, was captured and imprisoned in the Soviet Union for ten years. Sandor Rado, the Hungarian scientist who had confirmed Hitler's invasion date, was also jailed. He was imprisoned for eight years. Richard Sergei, the man who foresaw the German invasion and orchestrated an intelligence coup that sent Russian forces from the east to preserve Moscow, should have been a national hero. Stalin, though, turned down an offer to exchange him for a Japanese agent being imprisoned in

Moscow. Stalin delivered his address on the same day. The Japanese executed Sergei. During the years preceding WWII, Soviet intelligence was perhaps the best in the world; brave, devoted, and resourceful. Its agents were motivated mostly by idealism rather than Stalinist terror. In one of the sad ironies of Soviet history, many Russian intelligence agents were to discover that they were serving a tyrant who was as dangerous to them as any foreign enemy.

Chapter Six

The fall of a superpower - the fall of the Soviet Union

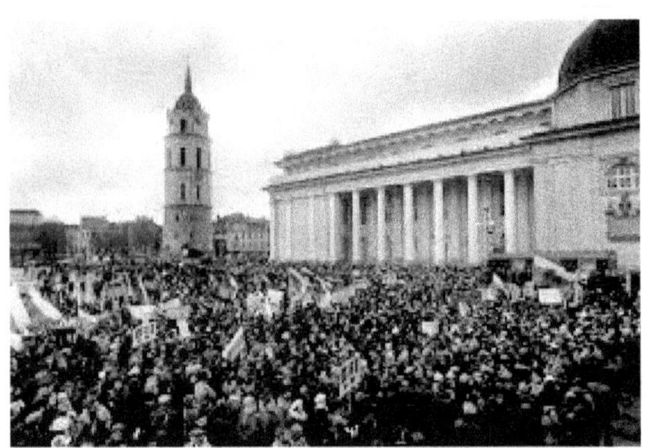

Moscow, 30 years after the Soviet Union's demise - The dazzling towers of a new commercial zone soar into the sky on the banks of the Moskva River, providing a confident picture of the new Russia. The crimson star of the Soviet Union still gleams above the Kremlin, and in Red Square in the Mausoleum, lays the leader of the October Revolution of 1917, Vladimir Lenin - the long lines in front of the Mausoleum may have vanished, but the Kremlin has remained the focus of power. It is led by Vladimir Putin, the Russian Federation's president. He rules over Russia, the world's largest country even without the former Soviet republics. A new government has long since taken over in the Kremlin, yet the old symbols remain as powerful as ever across the country. The former Soviet Union's legacy is complicated. The Soviet Empire occupied one-sixth of the earth's land area and housed 280 million people. The demise of this massive powerhouse in 1991 was unparalleled in history - a superpower abolishing itself. Since then, 15 new countries have struggled to find their position in the global system. Some have turned to Western Europe, while others have turned to China, but all are defined by their relationship with Russia.

The Russian flag now flies over the Kremlin instead of the crimson Soviet banner. The fall of the Soviet Union brought with it expectations for independence and prosperity for the former Soviet republics. But what is left of these streams? What does this newfound liberty entail? Which old disputes have resurfaced? Who has triumphed and who has suffered defeat, and what role does Russia play in the post-Soviet power struggle? At first glance, the Russian capital seems much like any other Western metropolis; consumerism is fashionable. Even in prosperous Moscow, though, the Soviet chapter of history has not been closed. The past has left an indelible imprint, prompting people to wonder what was good about Soviet times and what has changed for the better. Everyone assumed that because of democracy, things would continue to improve. Armenia is the smallest country in the world.

The former Soviet republics no longer have a border with Russia. New graves are continuously being erected in the military cemetery in Yerevan, Armenia's capital. They bore witness to the ongoing conflict and suffering. For decades, a persistent conflict has raged in the Caucasus between

Armenia and Azerbaijan, with both sides claiming the province of Nagorno-Karabakh, which has a majority Armenian population. Fighting over this mountain enclave dates back to Soviet times when both sides lost numerous lives in gun fights and pogroms. The wounds inflicted by the war are deep. Arvid Venisyan and his son Gevorg are Armenians living in Nagorno-Karabakh. They were soldiers, like their buddy Raya Haven, but they were not killed.

The most recent conflict ended in defeat, thanks in part to Azerbaijan receiving military assistance from Turkey. "The prospect of peace with their Azerbaijani neighbors has never seemed more remote than it does today," Arvid explained. It is no longer feasible, or at least quite unlikely, to coexist with such an opponent. The excitement and pride you observed on people's faces for the past 30 years have vanished. Their eyes no longer glitter. Much has changed. During the 44-day battle, no Western country took meaningful steps to assist us.

The Russian Army then entered the territories. The conflict was averted thanks to Russian assistance." In the summer of 2021, a shaky ceasefire between Armenia and Azerbaijan is in existence, and the border control post is overseen by Russian forces. Azerbaijan reclaimed substantial portions of Nagorno-Karabakh in 2021, forcing Armenia to cede the lost area. Long-term peace is a pipe dream. The locals identify as Armenian, and the country's flag is always flying. Today it seems serene, yet a year ago this was the front line when shots were fired. But, outside of the region, this conflict rarely registers, even though it has been raging on Europe's southern border for the past three decades. Azerbaijanis are Shiite Muslims, whereas Armenians are Christians. Their separate religions are a significant element of their national identities, which is one of the causes of the decades-long war. Armenia is a small country with a land area of only 30 000 square kilometers. The distance between the border and Yerevan, Armenia's capital, is short. Thousands were killed in the final major battle in 2020.

Thousands of soldiers are killed, many of whom are still very young, barely adults. The Caucasus conflict has had far-reaching implications. Turkey, a NATO member, backs the Muslim nation of Azerbaijan. France, on the other hand, is on the side of the Armenians. Russia is seeking to maintain its neutrality. After all, Moscow prioritizes its ties with oil-rich Azerbaijan. This is not how the Armenians anticipated their independence and freedom. Thirty years ago, fifteen Soviet republics achieved independence. They are part of Soviet territory one day and foreign countries the next. How can you regard Ukrainians as more foreign than Russians or Armenians and these areas as more alien? It's quite difficult. Foreign policy competence in the post-Soviet space is quite limited in Russia. Even the specialists recognize this. This sounds bizarre and contradictory.

For many years, they were part of the same country, yet the foreign ministry only has a few experts for Ukraine, Belarus, and the Caucasus. There are many more who focus on the United States, Germany, France, or the Benelux countries. A complicated legacy - despite the split, the old dependencies persisted. The whole infrastructure, including roads and railways, power lines, and oil and gas pipelines, was constructed to meet the needs of the Soviet Union and its centralized power base in Moscow. The

Institute of Economics of the Academy of Sciences is looking at the past and present links with Moscow. The institute's head, Ruslan Greenberg, is a long-time confidant of Mikhail Gorbachev who has come to a clear conclusion. "You have to understand that all post-Soviet republics have one single principle when it comes to their relationship with Russia, and it's been this way for 30 years - gaining maximum economic advantage from Russia while having a minimum of political commitments," he said. The Soviet Union was created in 1922 as a voluntary uniting of the Union Republics, at least according to the constitution. However, the right to secede from the union, much alone a withdrawal of all its members, had never been tested in practice. But that is exactly what happened in 1991: the country disintegrated into its constituent sections. The west was stunned by the quick disintegration, and 25 million Russians were stunned. They were thrown together by residents of other countries, exacerbated by the uncertainty of whether they would be accepted as citizens or allowed to keep their houses and land. The Center of German Studies is directed by Vladislav Belov. He is not Putin's political supporter, but he agrees with the president that the dissolution of the Soviet Union was the greatest geopolitical disaster of the twentieth century.

"One can agree with his stance," he said. If by geopolitics you mean the interests of specific people, and if we consider the fates of millions of people who, as a result of the unconstitutional dissolution of the USSR, found themselves trapped behind the borders of the country in which they thought they lived, I'm talking about 25 million Russian-speaking citizens who awoke one morning to find themselves living in another country. We are in one country now and will wake up in another tomorrow.

These folks were treated as second-class citizens, which is a disaster." Initially, attempts were made to repair the ruins. Following the Soviet Union's demise, the Torrid Palace and Saint Petersburg were to become the headquarters of the Commonwealth of the Independent States, a loose grouping of former Soviet republics. However, the three Baltic States, as well as Georgia and Ukraine, left or opted not to join, and the remaining states' commonwealth exists only on paper - no summits have been held in years. The CIS has no authority. Gerhard Mangold is an Austrian university professor and one of the world's foremost Russian experts. He also regards the CIS as a failed attempt to carry on the Soviet Union's legacy. "Under Yeltsin, there was undoubtedly the assumption that some kind of confederation would be conceivable," he remarked.

But, as Armenia's president put it at the time, this confederation of sovereign states was more like a vehicle for a peaceful divorce, and that's exactly what it was. It's astonishing that this organization still exists today, at least on paper, because no one wants to murder the baby by dissolving it totally, but it simply no longer has any practical political importance." The Baltic countries played an important role. Estonia, Latvia, and Lithuania were the first to secede from the Soviet Union and forge their path. Their relationship with Russia is strained. The Lithuanian capital of Vilnius the observation platform of the TV Tower is a renowned attraction in the capital. One can see how the city has changed from there. Around 50 000 new apartments have been created in the previous 20 years alone, more than any place else in the Baltic States. The country's parliament, known as the

Zema's since independence, is located in the center.

Ruslana's Baranovas is a philosophy graduate who works for a Social Democratic Party MP. "We've assimilated with the European Union and the West, and our living standards have improved," he remarked. Our borders were opened, and many Lithuanians fled to Western Europe, yet our fundamental concern remains inequality. Income inequality, uneven chances." Lithuania had 3.7 million inhabitants thirty years ago, but then the migration began. Nine hundred thousand Lithuanians fled the country, mostly young people, most of whom were well educated, to find work in the West, posing a major dilemma for this little republic. Despite this, both the capital and the country as a whole have embraced modernity. Annual economic growth has long been around three percent, and Lithuania boasts one of Europe's best fiber internet networks. Lithuanians, on the other hand, have a strong sense of national history and identity. Lithuania has long felt a part of the West; now on show at the Zamas is an exhibition commemorating the so-called Forest Brothers partisans who fought against Soviet occupation until 1953. Democracy might be taken for granted by the younger generation. Email Pasco climate studied educational science in Germany, but she has always called Vilnius home.

"I was just talking about this with my grandparents yesterday; we were evaluating what we had gained after 30 years of independence," she explained. My grandparents just mentioned one thing: we have the freedom to express ourselves and live in a free country. My generation and young people, in general, are frequently told - even my parents say it - that we don't know what freedom is because we've never lived in a country without freedom, that we can't appreciate what freedom means because we can just get on with our lives and believe this is normal and probably true." Emil is a member of Youth Debate, a group that aims to influence the political conversation in Lithuania. "Through our efforts," she explained.

Here in Lithuania, we arrange initiatives that are funded by the European Union, thus I live the European Union's principles every day. If I may say so, I feel myself to be more of a European citizen." Lithuania's ties to the West are growing stronger by the year. In 2004, the country joined Nato, along with its Baltic neighbors Estonia and Latvia, as well as four other former Soviet Union members. Military spending in Lithuania today accounts for about 2% of GDP. Nato conducted exercises in 2021, demonstrating a persistent fear of Russia, another remnant of the Soviet era.

However, the Baltic republics are home to a sizable Russian minority who refuses to reveal their ethnicity. Today, Russian influence takes a more hybrid form, such as control over television, which many people in Lithuania still watch, and influence over the internet. For many people, Russian is the only foreign language they know, so if they seek information beyond what Lithuanian TV and the internet provide, they will turn to Russian outlets. Lithuania regards Russia as a possible aggressor and expects Nato and the European Union to back it up. Even in the influential and critical publication Russia in Global Affairs, there is little sympathy for this position in Moscow. Nonetheless, Putin is showcasing Russia's military strength by conducting its maneuvers near the borders of Nato members, and tensions are rising on both sides.

Military parades in front of the Kremlin send a message to Russians that they should be proud of their force, while the West and Nato should be discouraged. According to Putin, the country is under siege, and its people must band together to defend it. Russia spent 4.3 percent of its GDP on defense in 2021. The army was humiliated, insulted, and underfunded, and its soldiers were left to hunger under Yeltsin. When Putin took office in 2000, it was like heaven on earth; there was peace and happiness, and now they have a powerful army and military vocations are once again coveted. All of this is part of the propaganda.

The old Soviet Union's imperial worldview survives in Russia today, legitimized by the red army's triumph over Hitler's Germany in World War II. 27 million people have died - The Great Patriotic War, as it is known in Russia, has left its mark on practically every Russian family, as well as Ukrainians, Belarusians, Kazakhs, and Kyrgyz. These recollections shape today's society as well. This conviction that Russians are a significant power capable of fending off hostile pressures and influences from the outside world is a fundamental aspect of their collective identity.

This confidence in the Soviet Union and Russia's unique authority and that they represent a special culture compensates for people's internal sentiments of dependence, poverty, and humiliation. What may appear weird to western visitors is normal to Russians. A painting depicting Georgie Shukov, the renowned Second World War general, proudly overlooking an inner-city commercial street is one example. This modern-day adoration of combat heroes sends another message: "never again will this once proud army portray such a humiliating image to the world as it did follow the Soviet Union's demise." Today Russia is displaying its power again, investing in new atomic weapons. The Soviet-era military-industrial complex is currently seeing a revival. However, the country as a whole is paying a high price. The political leadership believes that a 21st-century superpower must only define itself militarily, and Russia is only a superpower in military terms - not economically, monetarily, technologically, or demographically. The Russian people's purchasing power is expanding at a slower rate than practically anywhere else in Europe. Despite this, the Russian economy is expected to increase slightly, owing primarily to higher commodity prices.

Russia's businesses simply aren't inventive enough. There has been very little investment in infrastructure. Many of the country's transportation routes are in ruin. Russia still has only one highway connecting Moscow and Saint Petersburg. Their main transport link to the east, connecting Moscow and Beijing, is still under construction. Moscow has changed, but they want this to spread throughout Russia, with upgraded roads and infrastructure. The funds have vanished, but nothing has been built. Russia is now looking for strong partners, especially as relations with Western Europe have cooled. Russia and China are collaborating on the massive intercontinental project known as the New Silk Road. - Expectations for enormous earnings and expansion are strong. China is pursuing a cautious policy toward Russia by not actively making Russia feel like the junior partner, at least in economic and financial matters, because historically China has been and continues to be afraid that Russia can easily switch sides and align itself with the west, which should be avoided at all costs. To secure its historic zone of influence, Russia has refocused its attention on Central Asia.

The central Asian republics have largely welcomed this as a counterweight to China, their increasingly powerful neighbor. However, the opposite is true in Ukraine, where the majority of the population looks west rather than east. Ukraine was perhaps the greatest state in the former Soviet Union to make its independence a success. However, the country is currently in turmoil. President Volodymia Zelensky has failed to deliver on the promises of his people for peace and prosperity. Ukraine is become Europe's most corrupt country, making a formal alliance with Western Europe extremely impossible. While residents in western Ukraine overwhelmingly support joining Nato and the European Union, the east of the country, particularly Donetsk, feels a strong connection with Russia. Donbas, territories developed during the Soviet era, was home to rallies against the national administration in Kyiv. Fears of discrimination in a western-leaning nationalist Ukraine prompted a pro-Russian minority to take issue with the Ukrainian state. Ethnic Russians make up a significant proportion of the population; 8 million out of 42 million residents; and with Russia's support, these rallies developed into a separatist rebellion, a civil war that has rattled Europe and shows no signs of abating. In terms of language and traditions, Donbas was never Ukrainian.

The Crimean Peninsula in southern Ukraine became the site of an escalation in the Russian-Ukraine conflict in 2014. Today, Russia claims Crimea as part of its federation, and a massive new bridge connecting the Peninsula to the Russian mainland is being erected to convey a statement to the world: "We have taken back Crimea." It's a show of force directed at former Soviet states, demonstrating what will happen if they turn against Russia. Moscow orchestrated the massively successful. A separatist parliament has already been elected by the ethnic Russian population. This resulted in Russia annexing the territory.

Russia framed what Western Europe perceived as a gross violation of international law as a free decision by the majority of people in Crimea. This was a legitimate election; possibly not everything was done by international law, but it was not military occupation. There was no annexation. It was a public declaration of intent. It is difficult to find someone in Russia who does not regard Crimea to be a part of Russian territory. A new Russian patriotism emerged 30 years after the demise of the Soviet Union, maybe fueled by recollections of the country's former greatness. People were duped in the Soviet Union; those in charge promised one thing but delivered it on the other. It was a pretty simplified vision of what the future might hold. Everyone assumed that the excellent features of socialism would stay and that these advantages would be supplemented by two additional aspects.

First, consumer choice, followed by freedom, would result in perfect bliss. The transition from a socialist command economy to a capitalist market economy was abrupt and unexpected. The right to private ownership was not recognized under the Soviet regime. Even today, there is a strong link between property rights and enterprise in Russia, so picture what it was like back then. People who had previously been preoccupied with completely unrelated issues such as science or culture, but were suddenly compelled to become more determined to become business entrepreneurs to live and survive. Privatization was part of the shock treatment.

Privatization was chaotic and rushed without regard for the repercussions. Russia was thrown into a huge economic crisis at the end of the 1990s. Memories of this time are especially unpleasant for the elderly. The ruble was depreciated considerably, GDP was cut in half, child mortality reached scary new highs, and life expectancy was lower than in the third world – all while enormous corruption at the highest levels of authority existed. All of this has tarnished the concept of democracy and the mere name democracy in the eyes of the majority of Russians. Democracy was on the verge of becoming a filthy word. Because of people's experiences with the transition to an allegedly democratic government in the 1990s, and even today, studies from independent institutes show that only around a fifth of Russians want to live in a western-style democracy. But how do regular Russians feel about their country?

The Levada Center, one of the most well-known public polling agencies, frequently asks this question. Because the center is not under state authority, it is viewed with mistrust. When we asked Russians near the close of the Yeltsin administration what they expected from the next president, the majority indicated two wishes.
First, that the country would emerge from the economic crisis and achieve

an increase in living standards, and second, that Russia would be restored to the position of superpower that it held during the USSR, and Putin, with his demagoguery and rhetoric, as well as his strengthening of the military and the country's power structures, appeared poised to meet these expectations. Vladimir Putin's first term in government began in 2000, and he immediately tightened the screws on the country's strong oligarchs, signaling the beginning of a new era. He guaranteed that they would be able to conduct their businesses freely and that their enterprises would not be renationalized. In exchange, they promised him their undying loyalty. "Stay out of politics, and I will leave you in peace," he said.

The majority of Russians applauded. The current ruling party achieves its political goals through dominance, much as the former communist party did. It's like the old Yeltsin joke: "whatever party we build will always end up with the communists, so there's no alternative." On the other hand, the Russian political system and power structure are considerably more adaptable than the Soviet ones - they are capitalist. However, Russia is hardly the only country with a highly centralized authoritarian government. Consider Belarus, which is sandwiched between Russia and the European Union. Belarus was traditionally a solid friend of Russia due to their common history and languages, but this appears to be changing. The national flag, too, makes no secret the country's links to the Soviet Union. Only the hammer, sickle, and star remain. Reminders of the Soviet Union are everywhere, both in the capital Minsk and throughout the country. The country's economy is centrally located.
It is governed by a combination of corporate and governmental ownership,

and its lack of democratic structures and high levels of media censorship have won it widespread censure. Belarus has been a member of the EU since 1994. Alexander Lukashenko, a former Soviet political officer, has controlled the country indefinitely. Since his re-election in 2020, he has faced resistance.

His opposition to his government has grown louder. Hundreds of thousands of Belarusians have marched to the streets to demand democracy and the resignation of President Alexander Lukashenko. In Kazakhstan, too, an autocratic president has reigned for many years, but under different and more advantageous conditions than Russia. Because of its oil and gas reserves supplies, Kazakhstan is the region's richest country. In Soviet times, the Politburo of the Communist Party. Unlike Kazakhstan, the former Soviet republics of Uzbekistan, Kyrgyzstan, Turkmenistan, and Tajikistan struggled at first with their newfound independence. They were overly reliant on Moscow's centralized seat of power. Millions of individuals from Central Asian former Soviet republics have flocked to Russia as migrant workers, particularly to the cities of Moscow and Saint Petersburg. They work on construction sites, in the service industry, or agriculture. Meanwhile, Caucasians frequently operate as nomadic traders. Their earnings are typically the primary source of income for their families back home.

The majority of foreign workers are from Kyrgyzstan. Life in Bishkek, the capital, is shaped by both Islam and the legacies of the Soviet era. Everyone in the family works in Russia, whether it's the husband, wife, daughter, or son. Islam is a freshly resurrected pre-Soviet legacy in the country, and an enormous Russian Orthodox Church is nearby. National heroes from the past, as well as those from the more recent Soviet era, are adored. Kyrgyzstan has a population of 6.5 million people, 800,000 of whom are ethnic Russians. Along with Kyrgyz, Russian is an official language in this country. Under pressure from Muslim men, more and more women are refusing to work and prefer to stay at home and be housewives. Women's rights in the Soviet Union were better - women were more equal. Women are growing more religious, and they are wearing headscarves or veils. They are deafeningly deafening.

They no longer have an identity. Many Uzbeks live in the country's south. There have been outbreaks of violence between them and the Kyrgyz in the past, for a variety of reasons, including conflicting expressions of religious devotion. The Uzbeks adhere to a rigorous understanding of Islam, whilst the Kyrgyz are more moderate. In Kyrgyzstan, Islam can now shine once more.

In Jalalabad, the Imam is Uzbek, having completed his theology studies during the Soviet era. As Imam, the 66-year-old is not only a religious leader but also a sort of mayor in his neighborhood. "Life in the Soviet Union was good in my perspective," he remarked. Religious freedom existed, and religion was revered. The state remained neutral and respected religious borders. They didn't closely supervise us or tell us what to do - a proper religion was promoted. There were no terrorist organizations or bands back then, no thesis, Wahhabis, or Salafists, and we never advocated anything unlawful. We taught the faithful how to pray right and how to treat one another, but today there are more radical organizations, and the state must be more cautious." Kyrgyzstan considers itself to be a secular state. However, there is no telling how powerful an extremist form of Islam could grow.

Imam Madaliev preaches a moderate interpretation of Islam, and the Mosques are packed every Friday. In the atheist Soviet Union, the Imam worked as a civil servant and was paid every month. He now supports himself through the mosque's bakery and butcher shop. He accepts donations and operates a little farm. Even the Imam must go out to the fields after work every day to collect hay - this is the reality of life for a religious leader in Kyrgyzstan. "In the Soviet Union, everyone was equal, rich and poor were on the same level," he explained. Even as an Imam, I was paid 80 rubles each month. Everyone nowadays is split between rich and poor."

Corruption in our city has reached unprecedented heights; it is out of control. People in power are in power solely to enrich themselves, not to rule or benefit the country. They want to convert politics into a profit center for themselves. The ability of an NGO to publicly promote its ideals in this manner distinguishes Kirkus society from other Central Asian countries. Kyrgyzstan has far too few truly democratic parties. 78 different parties were running in the previous elections. Only three or four of them are democratic and liberal, which is worrying. That is why new political parties are so crucial.

The Russian army has long considered itself a guarantor of stability on the outskirts of this formerly multi-ethnic state. Since the fall of the Soviet Union, these border regions have been the scene of violent power battles, frequently involving Russian soldiers, as in the now-autonomous Czech Republic. Both the first and second Chechen wars were widely condemned by the general public. Around 55 to 65% of Russians considered these conflicts unjust and said they should be halted as soon as feasible. Anna Politkovskaya, a journalist, has been reporting for years on the cruelty of the Chechen conflict and corruption at the highest echelons of the Russian army. She was murdered in front of her Moscow apartment building in October 2006. Was her assassination ordered by political circles around the Kremlin, or was it the responsibility of the Chechen leadership? Despite trials and punishments, the true perpetrators were never identified. In Russia, the killing was interpreted as a warning to regime critics. But, if we look at the situation objectively, there is no strong opposition in Russia that could cause major problems for the Kremlin or be regarded as a threat. The principle of display power and smash descent works. This principle is reminiscent of Soviet power structures. The phrase "Homo Sovieticos" was coined in the 1960s to describe the Soviet citizen defined by conformist values and behaviors. Even today, many people in the former Soviet republics are formed by these essential beliefs. The Soviet citizen learned the skills necessary to live in a repressive regime.

He learned to deceive the state, accept its arbitrary decisions, and pretend to be devoted to it, all while dealing with his difficulties and attempting to survive in this harsh and restrictive atmosphere. Putin and his totalitarian system did not emerge by chance, but rather as a continuation of the Soviet dictatorship. There is only one significant distinction between the United States and the Soviet Union. Today, the blessing is not given by a single all-powerful party. Putin, a former communist party member, now has the support of a different authority: the Russian Orthodox Church. The church is not opposed to strengthening Russian conservative values When the Soviet Union's red flag was removed from the Kremlin thirty years ago, almost no one opposed it. The USSR had a population of 287 million people. Russia is the most populous of the successor states. It is still trying to find its place in the world between Europe and Asia. The last 30 years have been fraught with perplexity and difficulty. As a result, Russia has reclaimed its place as a global political player, but it is still a long way from where it could be with more imaginative leadership.

Russia is not attempting to imitate Western European-style democracy. Pride in Russia's magnificence, as well as an appeal to common traditions, are what will keep the country strong. That is why there is such nostalgia for one's childhood, for the school years, for our time as students, yet none of this has much to do with the Soviet Union. Putin was correct when he stated that "anyone who does not grieve the Soviet Union has no heart, but anyone who would return to what it was has no head." Thirty years later, the dreams of the past have given way to new realities; whether the Soviet Union's demise was truly a geopolitical disaster, or merely a new chance that some of its successor republics were hesitant to seize, only time will tell.

Chapter Seven

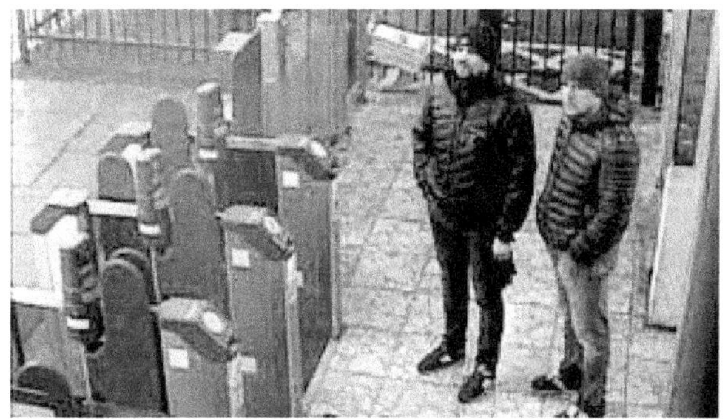

Christo Grozev of Bellingcat conducted the key investigation that allowed the crew of assassins to be identified as working for the Russian political police, the FSB, which is another version of the famed Soviet political police, the KGB. According to an investigation conducted by Christo and other journalists from Der Spiegel, CNN, and Navalny himself, the group of eight was dubbed the "Disgusting Eight" on the Russian internet. They attempted to assassinate Russian opposition leader Alexei Navalny, who was poisoned by a military nerve toxin from the Novichok group on August 20th, 2020 in the Russian Siberian city of Tomsk, which is about four hours' flight east of Moscow.

Colonel Stanislav Makshakov of the FSB Institute of Criminalistics appears to have coordinated this group of seven operatives. That was the one inquiry that Alexei Navalny turned into two clips that have now been viewed by over 50 million people. According to Christo Grozev's study, which was released only last week, almost the same gang of FSB assassins assassinated three more persons, two in the Russian caucuses, one a journalist, and another a human rights activist. The third person slain on the train was an activist who was formerly a Kremlin supporter. Christo is the serial killer who sits in the FSB or prison.

The Kremlin? In Moscow, though, there is a serial killer. That much we can be certain of. It's debatable if the serial killer works for the FSB or the Kremlin. It's a philosophical question rather than a practical classification. But there is undoubtedly a serial killer in Moscow, and it is a serial killer who operates on an industrial scale with delegation, not with his own hands, but through taxpayer-funded official agencies and structures to a degree not seen since the days of Stalin. This is nothing like for example, targeted assassinations or extraterritorial assassinations of terrorists or traitors carried out in the past by foreign intelligence services. This is something that targets dissidents and others who have not signed up for it.

People who are unaware that they could be on any kill list, according to the rules of engagement. This is extrajudicial, but more significantly, on a large scale. Because it is an organized murdering machine, calling it a serial killer is perhaps an understatement because a serial killer is restricted to their capability, whereas this is engaging the capability of a whole state. Vladimir

Putin, President of the Russian Federation, indicated that this probe was carried out by the CIA and other Western secret services. But how verifiable is this information? Why should we believe that information about their travel and communications is relevant to these assassinations? First and foremost, you must deal with some degree of probability.

You can never display orders issued by an FSB officer and signed by Russia's president; kill this and kill that. So, we must develop an assessment, which any prosecutor or court anywhere in the world would do based on representations from one side, one party, and the other. There is no investigation in this particular case. No country in the world wishes to investigate this case. A team of volunteers and open-source researchers act as if they are a prosecutor who does not exist.

As a result, we must examine the data holistically rather than from an individual degree of confidence in each component of the data. All of the data makes an image, and you may say that this convincing dataset of many different ingredients creates this picture, but this is not the case. You must have an alternate explanation or an alibi, and in this case, no one has been able to provide one. But how can we believe the data? Let's start with the data sources. They began using open-source data in Belling cat a couple of years ago. But then they started fighting against governments, or rather, investigating government criminality. Government crime is also difficult to uncover using only open-source data since governments can conceal open-source data. Following their initial examination of Russian military activity in Eastern Ukraine, which resulted in the shooting down of the Malaysian

Boeing MA17 with 298 people aboard, much of that research was based solely on open-source data of Russian servicemen leaving unintentionally.

They post photos with metadata to their social media sites. However, the Russian government banned the use of mobile phones in the army, which is just one example of how open-source material has become more difficult to obtain while investigating government-sponsored crime. They have to employ more than open-source data in this scenario. As a result, they relied on closed-source data. This included the suspects' travel and ticketing data for the previous ten years, as well as mobile phone data, which included not only the listing of phone call logs but also the geolocation and connection of each phone call to a specific base station - known as the broadcasting tower at any given time. This is data that they obtain via whistleblowers whenever possible, as well as from actual people working at mobile phone companies and even low-level police officers who are essentially selling this data without knowing to whom they are selling it through data brokers. We're now discussing the veracity of the data's legitimacy. They ensure the authenticity of data by using highly tight algorithms while working with it. First and foremost, they diversify the sources. None of the sources have any idea what they are working on.

They just have a segmented view of a specific request of one specific telephone number or one specific trip record of a specific person without knowing what context this is in. And they request data from at least two distinct sources for each piece of data they request so that they can verify if they match. And a critical component of the algorithm is that it attempts to match each piece of current data with historical data.

Let me give you an example. We were able to get highly thorough air flight ticketing data of all Russian nationals from 2014 to 2017 many years ago, three or four years ago. It was discovered on the dark web. We were able to obtain it. This includes around 75 million tickets sold during that period. And when we obtain, for example, in the context of the Navalny investigation, ticketing data for a specific suspect, we ensure that the data we obtain now is consistent with the data from the old data for the period 2014 to 2017. Because, even if someone tries to modify data today, they can't go back in time and manipulate the data from 2017. So these are just a few instances of how they ensure that the data is not tampered with. That is, in essence, why they believe in the data. The remainder, of course, is how they persuade readers to believe the statistics. In this case, the findings they stumbled upon, which is that there is a machine a government-run machine to kill people, were so implausible that they needed to engage many international media with their reputation so that they could convince the audience that this is not just a crazy guy or a crazy team Bellingcat manufacturing data.

So they enlisted the help of CNN's "Der Spiegel," Spain's "El Pais," and our Russian traditional partner "The Insider." And they simply handed them this data and said, "Look at it." We won't tell you what we discovered, but take a look at these, these, and these dates and tell us what you see first. Second, you must validate the data yourself. "Reach your conclusions" on the veracity of this material, and "ask us if you have any questions." So, for a week, these media organizations sat down together, or not all together, but some of them were in the same room together, poring over hundreds of pages of records, scratching their heads, and occasionally cursing because what they saw was so unbelievable. However, this is only one example of how they operate with data and why they believe everything they have established is validated. But where was the breaking point? Alexei Navalny was allegedly poisoned in a hotel in Tomsk before boarding the plane, where he slumped on the floor near the plane's restroom two hours later. The pilot of S7 quickly landed at Omsk, which is a two-hour flight from Tomsk, and so he did. On the field, the ER collided with the plane.

Navalny was given atropine in the ER car. So we feel that these two things, which many of the individuals who wrote about believe that the pilot of the Russian airline S7 and the air doctor essentially saved Navalny's life. Navalny was then transported to a hospital in Tomsk. He was already in a coma, and Putin allowed Navalny to be transferred to Germany via airlift in two days. So, when did the probe reach a breaking point? There were numerous tipping points because they first had a strong working theory that they located the would-be killers with the correct motive, means, and method. And this came when they found that three others had flown on parallel flights, not on the same trip as Navalny, but just before Navalny to the city of Novosibirsk in Eastern Russia. And then five days later, one day after Navalny, he bought tickets back from Tomsk to Moscow. So imagine the seemingly unlikely coincidence of someone purchasing a ticket to Novosibirsk on August 13th and then returning to Tomsk on August 21st, overlapping with Alexei Navalny's and his team's planning.

As a result, this was their first strong hypothesis. But the breaking point came when they discovered that two of the three people, they discovered on these flights had a phony identity and were traveling under names that didn't exist in real life. And the third, who traveled under his true name, discovered that he had traveled on parallel flights with Alexei Navalny 11 times in the previous five years, with the majority of them occurring in 2011. Then they discovered that on the same booking as this individual, FSB officer Vladimir Panyaev, there had been six other people who frequently flew with him to the same place.

They discovered that two of these had nearly identical names and birth dates to the two phony identities that accompanied him to Tomsk. They were able to obtain images of those folks while using both phony and actual identities. They recognized these individuals. Then they broadened the universe of flights that they could compare to one another. Since 2017, we've been flying Navalny to various Russian destinations till his coma in 2020. Then there were these seven persons whom they knew were somehow connected because they flew together frequently.

They compared those trips to Alexei's flights and discovered 37 overlapping flights. Anyone who has studied statistics, even if they haven't completed Statistics 101, knows that the likelihood of this being a coincidence is almost none. It's near zero, but it's an outright impossibility. That was the decisive moment when they realized this was the team. There is no reason for this not to be the team. But then they discovered that of this team of seven people, four were medical professionals, two were chemical weapons specialists, and one was a member of the CIA.

The FSB's Department for the Protection of Constitutional Order is Russia's political police. In modern Russia, this is the counterpart of the Gestapo. It is a branch of the FSB whose sole purpose is to protect and sustain the current system. As it was known in the Soviet Union as the defeat director, the Second Service is now directed by General Smirnov. As a result, these people always flew together. They flew with Alexei Navalny on around 10% of their flights over the last five years. And, of course, the first thing they do is try to abandon the innocent notion or hunt for an innocent explanation. Of course, the innocent answer in this situation was that, well, everyone knows Russia is a police state. Perhaps these were just folks following Navalny to see what he was up to. So that may have been pure surveillance. Wrong. A team of doctors and chemical weapons experts cannot explain this.

The same squad was always following him, which defied any reasonable observation. Because multiple teams should be following up, adjusting, and replacing in surveillance. You've all seen espionage movies, so you understand how it works. And in surveillance, you always have them on the same flight because else you miss a large portion of the objective. In their instance, they always went on various aircraft either behind or ahead of him to avoid being identified. They also discovered that they never followed Alexei Navalny on a trip where he did not stay in a hotel.

So, if he flew to a city for the day and returned in the evening, they would never buy a ticket for that. They'd simply ignore it. But they tracked him on every single journey he did in 2017, which is significant because that was the year he ran for President or wanted to run for President but was not allowed, and on every single trip he took where he had a stayover. The fact that they did not follow him on day outings also contradicts the innocent idea that he was simply being watched. Then, significantly, and this was the final straw, they discovered that these doctors and chemical weapons specialists were communicating via phone with a Russian institute named the Scientific Center Signal. It is the Signal Institute, which is staffed by 12 past or present professionals in the field.

The old chemical weapons Military Institute Number 33 of the Ministry of Defense, which tested Novichok and 21 other chemical weapons in the 1970s, 1980s, and 1990s There is no credible innocent explanation for why the crew that tailed Navalny for a total of 37 flights has suddenly increased the flight number to 41 because they didn't know some names when they announced this. So, throughout the days and during the time that they were in Tomsk and Novosibirsk, medical physicians and chemical weapons specialists would be interacting with an institute that only specialized in producing Novichok and other chemical weapons on 41 separate flights. Any court and any jury of jury members, any prosecutor in the world would agree that this is a convincing comprehensive case and that the guilt is on these guys.

The final straw in terms of explaining our belief in getting to the result, and the final tipping point, was when they were eventually able to obtain the phone records of one of the doctors on the team who accompanied Navalny. And they expected him not to have turned on his phone while on a mission like that. This was his phone, and he would communicate through other means. But when we talk about individuals, there is always a margin for human mistake, and in this case, they were fortunate to come upon that fault. That's when this individual turned on his phone for a split second. The only explanation, it appears, is to look at a number he didn't know by heart. The phone merely exchanged one byte of data with the base station. This data placed him approximately a 20-minute walk from the hotel where Alexei Navalny had just gone to bed that evening before waking up, heading to the airport, and slipping into a coma a few hours later. This is a list of the tipping points in order. Three additional victims were allegedly assassinated by the same group of assassins.

The Kremlin or the FSB would entrust such an illegal technique of killing and information about this illegal operation to more than one team, both under international law and under Russian law. So there is only one team. But what they witnessed in the three successful operations so far was the presence of at least two members of this wider team at the location of the suspicious death by poisoning in all three cases. They feel there is more. There are other members of this team they haven't identified yet, or more different phony identities they don't know about yet? However, the presence of at least two members of this team in each of the three incidents is sufficient for them to attribute those suspicious deaths to this operation as well.

So, there is this gang of assassins from the military intelligence group who carry out assassinations outside of Russia and another group who carry out assassinations within Russia. There is some overlap between the two groups, and it is under the means and technique. They both employ Novichok frequently, but not always. Other poisons are used by the FSB for less significant targets, but the method is the same.

The Signal Institute supplies Novichok to both the GRU and the FSB. That is what they have been able to demonstrate by monitoring the communication pattern. Both the GRU and the FSB murder teams consult with The Signal Institute scientists before embarking on an operation. It was recently revealed that one of the doctors treating Alexei Navalny in Omsk died unexpectedly at the age of 55. Sergei Maksimishin was his name. He oversaw Intensive Care at the Omsk hospital where Alexei Navalny was being treated for two days.

"A doctor who was in charge of treating "Alexei Navalny in Russia shortly after he was poisoned," according to the "Daily Mail." They believe he was assassinated as well. Coincidences happen, and it would be against the Kremlin's self-interest to carry out such an obvious assassination of someone who would be quickly ascribed to the Kremlin by the "Daily Mail" or the global media. However, that was based on an instinct we had earlier to predict the likelihood of a crime occurring, which was included in this algorithm of the instinct and the reputation cost for the Kremlin. Since this investigation, as well as what has happened in the last two weeks with the protests in Moscow and the arrest of thousands of people, including journalists, we believe that the Kremlin has completely ignored the concept of reputation cost, and we should not be surprised if this is what happened.

They have seen that the same poison squad that we discussed traveled to Omsk, the location of the hospital, not only in the immediate aftermath of the poisoning for which they earned an award but also in subsequent years.

The explanation was provided by a confession by one of the poison team members who stated that they went there in August and September to wipe up the traces of the evidence However, they discovered that members of this team visited Omsk in October and December of 2020. That would no longer make sense from the standpoint of removing traces. So the question is whether there was already a strategy in place to dispose of some of the witnesses. This appears to be insane and not in the Kremlin's best interests, but we are no longer convinced that the Kremlin is only concerned with its reputation. There is speculation that Navalny and his wife Yulia were poisoned in the past and survived. We can't say with the same surety that they were poisoned. What they rapidly discovered was that Alexei and his wife went to the Russian town of Kaliningrad for a romantic holiday a month and a half before the final nearly deadly journey for Alexei. And they discovered that the same poisoners, as well as the same team of FSB personnel, had flown to Kaliningrad just a few hours before Alexei and his wife arrived.

They stayed till the fourth day of their romantic vacation. On the sixth day, they returned to Moscow. Yulia Navalny felt extremely identical symptoms to Alexei's poisoning symptoms a month and a half later, except they were weaker, which might be explained by her being accidentally exposed to a smaller quantity, according to numerous chemical weapons professionals with whom they consulted. After discovering that the most likely way of administration of the poison was through Alexei Navalny's underwear, where the murder crew was able to reach and place the poison, it is possible that Yulia came into touch with poisoned underwear or clothes Alexei Navalny. But it was only for a brief period, and she was not exposed to a lethal quantity of it. The same team is there, as is a member of the family who is suffering from severe poisoning symptoms. One of the original designers of the military nerve agent Novichok stated that the poison was not intended to kill individuals but rather "some persons like a battalion on the battlefield." "It was to be inserted," that is Novichok, "in something like a grenade and launched towards the enemy."As a result," he claimed, "it was difficult to identify the exact quantity "appropriate to poison to death" for the alleged FSB assassins." He suspects the assassins were testing poison on others, including Navalny, to determine the deadly dose.

However, many chemical weapons experts, including former staff of the Organization for the Prohibition of Chemical Weapons, believe that Novichok does pose an issue when supplied individually in the amount since if you apply too little, the victim would only experience discomfort. This is because Novichok fundamentally affects your nerve connectors, and the body, like the internet, can redirect its nerve connections even if nearly 90% of the nerve connectors are destroyed.

So, if you misapply and use a low amount, the victim will detect but not realize they've been poisoned. And if you, do it with an overdose with a substantial amount, the individual may die immediately, which would too easily link the crime to the offenders. Furthermore, it risks repercussions for the poisoner himself or herself. As a result, determining the proper dosage is extremely challenging. As a result, a long-term testing method is required. Whether they did it to animals or not. This is not achievable correctly, or on inmates or real targets, we're not sure, but on someone who must have tested it. Vil Mirzayanov, one of the Novichok's creators, believes that human targets were exploited when the poison was being developed during the Soviet era. Christo Anna Politkovskaya, on the other hand, was slain with a bullet. The same thing happened to Boris Nemtsov, who was slain just a few hundred meters from the Kremlin, and Mark Kramer, who is the head of the Davis Center's Cold War Studies Center. "Why do Kremlin officials rely on poisoning?" "Occasionally, the poison kills the target," but not always. "When Ramzan Kadyrov wants someone dead," Mark suspects, "he tells his assassins to shoot the target," a strategy that almost always works. "Why doesn't the Kremlin use firearms instead of poison?" Because of plausible deniability.

When dealing with high-level opposition leaders or high-profile people in general, there is a necessity for deniability. One type of Ramzan Kadyrov is all about denial. Until recently, theories regarding Nemtsov are most likely unknown. Politovska's likely motivations have shifted after the Navalny investigation. Previously, they believed that Russian power figures such as Ramzan Kadyrov or even oligarchs were attempting to deliver a gift to the Kremlin that was probably not even desirable for the Kremlin because the Kremlin could not benefit from this balance of reputation cost versus getting rid of a nuisance such as Nemtsov. But we now believe that the Kadyrov route was only one of several options for a covert killing. "We're sad it wasn't us." It was just a bunch of wild Chechens." Similarly, successful poisoning via poison can be used to achieve deniability. What they see today are three cases that they believe is the result of an FSB assassination campaign, and no one knew or could show they were poisoned by the government. Everyone assumed it was the result of natural causes or a local opponent. So it's similar in that it's debatable. Either by doing it in a way that can always be written off as a natural course or by using a bullet but doing it in the hands of someone whom we can swear is not us.

Chechnya's leader was Ramzan Kadyrov. His father was a well-known sheik in Chechnya before the war in the 1990s. So, he grew up essentially among guerillas with guerillas, and when Putin became president, he made peace with Chechnya, and Ramzan Kadyrov became the willing executioner of what Putin wanted from him - the enforcer. But how did they track down the suspects? It was accomplished by combining two ends of their inquiry. One was looking for the poison, while the other was looking for humans. Tracking the poison entails following phone calls made by scientists from The Signal Center because another study on the GRU revealed that these scientists developed the Novichok. So, they observed that they spoke with certain FSB members. They then put that on hold for a time because they didn't know which branch of the FSB these members belonged to. On the other hand, they searched through the travel records of persons who flew with Navalny, and long story short, they discovered an overlap between six people whom both spoke to The Signal Institute and traveled with him. Navalny. These six people became the foundation of their identity.

They had never traveled with Navalny. Some performed surveillance, but the assassins who were identified never flew on the same plane with Navalny. They hypothesized that it was because they didn't want to be seen tracking him for an extended period. But, as Yevgenia mentioned, this was confirmed in a phone call, but Alexei Navalny called one of his prisoners after they presented him with their findings in a prank call, and he was able to get him to talk for 50 minutes under the guise of reporting to an upper-security official about the failed operation on Navalny himself. And this person said in that 50-minute call that they never traveled with Navalny to avoid being observed. First, Navalny released the findings of Christo and others' investigation. Following the release of the first footage, Vladimir Putin, President of Russia, held a press conference. He was also questioned about the probe. He stated that, of course, it's all BS and that there's nothing real about these. And who cares about Navalny, and he never even refers to him by name? What does it matter? Who is he to deal with, he said? And if we wanted to poison or murder him, we would undoubtedly get the job done, declared Russian Federation President Vladimir Putin. He did validate a large portion of their findings during that news conference. "Yeah, I'm aware of that probe," he responded. And, of course, there were FSB officers following him. "He's a spy; he's an enemy of the state," he says, "and he should expect to be watched."

Vladimir Putin made that comment on Thursday, and the following Monday, Navalny released another video in which he purported to be an aide to General Nikolai Patrushev, Putin's former KGB comrade and now the head of the Russian Security Council, one of the current Kremlin's stars. So

Navalny pretended to be his assistant and said he was creating a report for Mr. Patrushev that needed to be completed fast. It had been a long night. So he began questioning this agent, and this operative admitted that apparently poison was placed in the codpiece of Navalny's underwear.

That was a fantastic piece of investigation that stunned the Kremlin. Putin intends to implement procedures to reduce that danger by having, for example, access to chemical weapons and large-scale explosives subject to two signatures from two distinct agencies: one from the FSB and one from the FSO, Putin's direct secret service. This is being followed by intelligence services. This could change if Putin becomes too much of a thorn for the elite, and the elite can persuade some of the security top brass to switch sides. It's already happened, and the Russians rule it. It's a corporate state, and it's run by a corporation of KGB grads. There are also those civilians whose job is to write a column daily. These types of regimes are well known in political science, particularly in Latin America.

They are referred to as bureaucratic-military authoritarian regimes. But did the detectives know ahead of time "what you would be able to extract from the phone call," or was it a shot in the dark? So, there was no chance. The plan was entirely different. The goal was for Alexei to meet his assailants and say, "Hi, my name is Alexei Navalny. "You may remember me "from the time you tried to kill me. "Why did you do that?" That was the plan all along. It was simply a moral obligation for him to do so, but he modified the script in the middle of the prank call.

He experimented on two persons. The first one responded, "No, you're not a Patrushev assistant. "I know exactly who you are." He then hung up. And the second was completely unexpected. For the first three minutes, they felt this person was just playing a game to keep Navalny going for whatever purpose. They even expected the Russian FSB to appear in the room where they were in Germany and shut the door. But the tipping point came when this same officer revealed additional information that they didn't have before. Then they realized it was real. This guy thinks he's speaking to the boss's helper.

This new information was connected to the fact that he was cleaning the codpiece at the time the poison was placed there. That's one, and the second is that he gave them names they didn't know about. He supplied the identity of the local FSB officer from the Constitutional Protection Unit in Omsk who was snatching Navalny's hospital clothing and delivering them to him. As a result, this was new information for them. But, more importantly, he confirmed our understanding of why Navalny lived. Because Alexei Navalny asked him, among other things, why he failed. Then he mentioned circumstances.

The pilot landed the jet too soon, and the paramedics on the landing strip treated him incorrectly. As a result of these two negative developments, it did not work in our favor. This was the first time they had heard someone mention death prevention as a negative development. But what exactly is the Disgusting Eight's job description? Is there a specific individual who put the poison in Navalny's underwear at the Tomsk hotel? Based on the overlap of people in different poisoning efforts, they can be certain that the critical people are Alexey Alexandrov and Ivan Osipov, two medical physicians who have worked in this facility since 2010, more than ten years already, and have gone from helping people to killing them. It's a classic case of gently boiling the frog. They were initially given targets that appeared plausible to them. They were given real terrorist targets during the second Chechen War, and there were terrorist attacks on Russian citizens in the aftermath, therefore they were ordered to assassinate terrorists.

Then, gradually, this entire institute of this death machine was added to the lawful targets with more and more personal corporate interests, and these guys only missed the moment when they became killers for hire for President Putin. But who ordered the assassination or attempted assassination of Russia's opposition leader?

There are handwritten minutes written by Pavel Sudoplatov, the head of the chief assassin in the Stalinist era, one of those who were preparing the assassination of Lev Trotsky along with his deputy Eitingon and who was involved in several other assassinations, including one of the American citizens Oggins back in the post-World War II period. When Khrushchev succeeded and became the head of the country, Sudoplatov and some of Stalin's subordinates were imprisoned and sentenced to 15 years in prison. He was imprisoned for 13 years. He was then released. And at the end of his life, he had been largely rehabilitated.

However, what is significant about these memos is that Sudoplatov writes about people who gave him instructions The order to assassinate this or that individual was almost often delivered by Stalin, the then-leader of the Soviet Union, or by Molotov, the minister of foreign affairs and afterward the chief of government, or by both of them. So, in every case, it was the leader of the Soviet state who gave the order. Several KGB sources kept saying that after Stalin died, it was the General Secretary of the Communist Party and we know that Khrushchev himself ordered the assassination of Bandera and then another person that it was the leader of the country who gave this order because only the leader of the country could provide some sort of guarantee to the executioner to enforcer. Given this, do we believe Putin, the President of the Russian Federation, gave the order to assassinate Navalny? We don't know if he came up with the notion first, or if Patrushev or someone else came up with it. Let's kill him so no one knows."

However, many people are certain that Putin approved it for the same reasons as an example from Soviet times, as well as for another. Both Stalin and Putin are anxious about their circle and authority, thus handing an extrajudicial tool with some degree of self-sufficiency poisoners to others to select whom the target runs counter to this paranoia. He would never let this unit determine whom to poison on its own. He would never allow them to obtain the genuine poison for this particular operation without his signature, simply because if he didn't, one day he might be on the receiving end. All of this makes it impossible for Putin to have approved every single operation.

The question is whether he can handle so many approvals. Based on travel statistics, we predict that these people kill or attempt to kill 8 to 10 people per year. So, certainly, he can do it. As a result, they judged that the public's interest in understanding and trusting this data outweighed their ability to continue working. And they know, and they have previously encountered problems in continuing their studies, but this was the tipping point where they had to say enough is enough and convince the world that this is what is happening in modern society.

Will the Kremlin continue to rely on Novichok and the specific assassins now that Bellingcat has made these facts public, and what will happen to those assassins? Unlike during Stalin's reign, we have not witnessed actual executions as a result of mistakes in today's Russia. We've seen betrayal-related homicides, but not mistakes. So, they will be punished by being sent to a desk job in a fascinating section of Russia, but they will not be imprisoned or killed.

The question is whether they will be able to replace them soon enough. And the benefit of their open probe is that they cannot envisage anyone - any doctor - now accepting the job offer and assuming that it can be kept hidden indefinitely. For the next ten years, the current impact of their probe will make it extremely difficult for the Kremlin to re-employ people. But is there any explanation for how the FSB poisoner was so readily duped during the fake call? Well, if you speak Russian, you'll probably find it easier to believe than if you don't because Alexei Navalny is an excellent actor. He was able to replicate not just the FSB's military system's speech pattern and terminology, but also their bullying method. His speech was riddled with parasite phrases such as "you know what the boss is expecting," "you know that I need to perform," and "you know what will happen to me." And this guy felt sympathy for Alexei, whom he saw as the boss's aide.

In addition, he was bullied. So, he felt both bullied and empathetic at the same time, and it was the time constraint "I need this by eight or we're both in danger" that succeeded. Alexei was a fantastic actor that morning. It also pretty well reflects the psyche of Russian bureaucrats. Someone from the big boss's assistant to the general called and questioned him. He was probably boosted by the fact that Patrushev himself requested information from him. "I'm calling you first before I contact your boss," Alexei continued, "since I got the good word about you from the top person." "He knows me in person?" he said. And Alexei confirmed that Bogdanov knows him in person. This worked, and this chemical weapons specialist was probably not that bright because he asked on an open line.

"But is it okay if we talk on an open line?" After that, on an open channel "Oh yes, it is acceptable to chat in an open line," Alexei replied. So, this vicious spiral didn't occur to him as a feasible topic of conversation. Another thing that reveals something about Russian bureaucracy. Protocol, conventions, and norms are far less significant than the hierarchy or a directive from a superior.

This is an incredible opportunity for anyone interested in Russian bureaucracy, a psychological case study, or a Ph.D. But to what extent was it ethical to pay money for information obtained on the dark internet? It's rather common among European journalists. Journalists in most of Europe, much of Western Europe, Italy, France, and even sometimes in the United Kingdom pay for information, particularly those in tabloids. However, over the Atlantic in the United States, the following is the line of thought. If you pay for the knowledge, the person who is delivering it will feed you a frenzy only to collect your money. There are numerous reasons not to. The one that does not apply in this circumstance is because the ones selling this information have no idea why they are providing it. They have no idea what the information is about. They do not know the subject. They are unaware of the names for which they are providing information. And they're merely in the information trading industry to make quick cash. So it's simply a matter of whether we choose to embrace that knowledge and that ethical bargain, and it's all in the public interest. If Russian investigators chose to look into this crime, they could simply get this information without spending any money. They're not going to investigate a crime committed by their president, so that's out. What is the other option?

For a foreign government to look into? Nobody wants to do it because it means crossing the line of national sovereignty. Germany does not want to look into a crime that occurred in Russia. They have stepped into the shoes of investigators. They do not have access to international databases. They must purchase the data, which they do. And, of course, the Russian government and law enforcement authorities declined to even open a criminal investigation into the alleged assassination attempt on Alexei Navalny. This is also true a very telling fact Why did Navalny return to Russia knowing he would be arrested? He was already decided to return in the middle of January. And he just stated, "I know I may be arrested." I'm afraid I'll be killed. But if I stay here, I will never be able to help Russia. I'll never be able to be a politician because I'll be written off as one of the many emigrants within a couple of months" he wanted to be a politician, not a journalist and that's a difference and he needs to be where his potential electorate is and the unique thing about him is he's willing to pay the price of staying in jail for a year or two just knowing that one day he'll be out hopefully and few people are capable of doing so. But is it possible that Navalny will be murdered in prison? That is a result of the newly discovered insight that there is no reputation cost that the Kremlin is unwilling to pay. As a result, they may fare even worse.

They may torture him or simply attempt to induce a mental collapse for him in jail, which in certain situations may be worse than death. There were examples like that in the Soviet era. One of them was a dissident named Morozoff, who was duped by the KGB into revealing several names. Several people were arrested. Morozoff committed suicide in his cell. Another case in point was the legendary dissident Mergensana, who went on hunger strike and died in prison. What options are there? In reality, what kind of pressure should be applied? What can we do to get Navalny to leave? Well, this is a quantum leap above anything we've seen previously. We are witnessing a systematic killing machine, and it is not enough for governments to voice worry as has occurred thus far. It is time to approach the Russian government similar to the North Korean administration, at least temporarily. It is a terrorist regime, and it must be considered as such by everyone. Our citizen job as non-government officials are to explain to the passive part of the population.

There is a populace that is not aware of what is going on, and it is a different Russia than the Russia we wanted to be friends with even 15 years ago. What kind of sanctions can we expect from Western countries in retaliation for the assassination attempt on Alexei Navalny? We anticipate that the institutes recognized as it should be legal to manufacture Novichok these days. We also anticipate that the whole list of Institute of Criminalistics employees will be approved. But that will not work to change the system. What Alexei Navalny has proposed is going after close supporters and friends of President Putin who keep his money and making them feel like he's a hot potato for them, and generating the change from inside by genuinely people stopping to be proxies for President Putin.

www.ingramcontent.com/pod-product-compliance
Lightning Source LLC
LaVergne TN
LVHW020914200726
843506LV00011B/1712